Dear Stefania: Thank you very much. I hope you enjoy the book - ... smiling.

Finding Your S·M·I·L·E·

Anthony Pennimpede CA

AP3 MEDIA

www.AP3media.ca www.AP3media.com

National Library of Canada Cataloguing in Publication

ISBN 978-0-9784772-0-2

This book is designed to provide accurate and authoritative information on the subject of performance management. While all of the stories and anecdotes described in the book are based on true experiences, some situations have been changed slightly to protect each individual's privacy. It is sold with the understanding that neither the author nor the publisher is engaged in rendering legal, accounting, or other professional services by publishing this book. As each individual situation is unique, questions relevant to performance management specific to the individual should be addressed to an appropriate professional to ensure that the situation has been evaluated carefully and appropriately. The author and publisher specifically disclaim any liability, loss or risk which is incurred as a consequence, directly or indirectly, of the use and application of any of the contents of this work.

Both the Canadian and U.S. edition of this book were published by AP3 Media.

Visit AP3 Media's website: **www.AP3media.com**

Acknowledgements

I would like to thank my wife, Josee, for always being there for me, supporting me in countless ways whenever necessary and for putting up with me (which is not always easy to do). The inspiration for this book struck me during our honeymoon in Hawaii. Although Josee laughed at me when I first told her the idea for my book shortly after our honeymoon, her faith, trust and patience helped me complete what was an amazing experience.

I would also like to thank my parents Frank and Maria who have supported me throughout my life. My parents have always been there for me and I hope I will be as warm, generous and loving with my children as my parents were with me. Their endless love and kindness are proof yet again that I am blessed with the best parents in the world.

I also must thank my brother Marco and my sister Sonia for being there for me. Marco's wit and logic and Sonia's wisdom and thoughtfulness are priceless. It is an honour to be their older, geeky brother.

Thanks to my family and my wife's family for being supportive and caring. Life would be incomplete without our famiglia (family).

A special thanks to my professional team consisting of Kathe (editor), Rami (designer), Rakesh (photographer) and Gianfranco (lawyer) who contributed their skills and helped make my dream a reality. It was an absolute pleasure to work with such a fantastic team.

Finally, to my best friends from RDP and elsewhere (you know who you are). I am proud to have each and every one of you in my life and to call you my friends.

With much love,

Anthony

About the Author

Who is Anthony Pennimpede?

Introduction

I am a Canadian of Italian origin, born and raised in Montreal, Quebec (Canada). I am blessed with amazing parents, a terrific brother, and a splendid sister. I am married to a wonderful woman. I have a fabulous family and a superstar group of friends.

I am a Canadian Chartered Accountant (equivalent to a CPA in the United States—Certified Public Accountant). I successfully completed my undergraduate studies from McGill University in Montreal and my graduate studies from Concordia University, also in Montreal. I obtained my Chartered Accounting designation from the Order of Chartered Accountants of Quebec in 2003.

What do you need to know about me when reading this book?

Everything I do in life involves a struggle. I've always had to work harder than my peers in both my academic and professional careers to achieve modest results. I am no superstar. I am no genius. I'm not blessed with superhuman strength (I suffer from migraines) nor with superhuman skills (I can't concentrate for long periods of time, find it difficult to focus, and can't stay awake when I try to study or work late). I am one of those middle-of-the-pack people.

To overcome those "temporary" hurdles (migraines, lack of super-talent), I always try my best, work hard, and strive until completion. I take nothing for granted. I am grateful for all life has to offer me. Regardless of how I may look "on paper," I am committed, ambitious, stubborn, humble, and willing to work hard to achieve anything.

Anthony's Message

Purpose

This book is for those who are searching for more. The "more" you're looking for could mean getting more from your career, more from your relationships, or simply getting more out of your life. This book, in conjunction with the website (www.AP3media.com), will help you find what you're searching for (the thing you want "more" of). It will help you discover your hidden potential, develop that extra self-confidence, and improve your life. The tools I share with you will help you achieve your goals and serve as your guide on your path to success.

What is success?

Success can mean different things to different people. Success may be specific or general in nature. Specific success may take the form of an achievement ($1 million in personal net worth, a job promotion, achieving your target weight). It's relatively easy to know once you have achieved your specific success.

General success is a state of mind in which you have everything you believe to be important in your life (a wonderful spouse, a loving family, beautiful children, best friends, an interesting career).

I believe that in order to be truly successful, you must seek both specific and general success. How great is it to know that you are financially stable, have a promising career, are in the best physical shape of your life, and have wonderful people (spouse, family, friends) to share all this with? True success means having achieved both specific and general success.

You must be able to S.M.I.L.E.
S.M.I.L.E. = Success Means I Love Everything

You must believe that true success means you love everything about your life. You love your spouse, family, friends, and most importantly, yourself. "Yourself" meaning who you are (general success), what you possess (specific success), and what you have achieved in your life (both general and specific success).

This book will help you achieve success in your own terms. This book will help make your dreams a reality.

I am convinced that if you:

1. want to succeed;
2. set out to be the best you can be;
3. and devote your best effort to achieving your goals
...then you will achieve SUCCESS.

Your MISSION, should you choose to accept it, is to:

- **identify your goals;**
- **challenge yourself to achieve your goals; and**
- **promise yourself to continue striving, grinding, and working until you do achieve them.**

Use these tools (this book, the website) to succeed. Witness the effects of achieving your success (your goals) on your life and the lives of everyone around you. Amaze yourself with the potential you know you have inside you. And enjoy the rewards of having fulfilled your dreams.

I guarantee you the journey will be worthwhile.

Before You Begin

Why read this book?

If you're reading this book, then I assume there's something in your life you want to improve. Let this book be your guide, companion, and road map to success and self-fulfillment. Before you embark on your journey, make sure you have all the tools you'll need. This book is your starting point and primary source of inspiration and guidance. I have also set up a website (www.AP3media.com) with valuable resources as a complement to this book. I hope you'll find both the book and the website useful.

You've already taken the first step towards your dreams. Your quest for success has officially begun. Never lose sight of your mission:

To find your S.M.I.L.E. (Success Means I Love Everything)

This book and the resources available on the website will help you find your S.M.I.L.E. You've read famous people's success stories—now it's time to create your own.

Good luck!

Table of Contents

Introduction

I have good news and excellent news.

Here's the good news: as the old saying goes, there are only two guarantees in life (death and taxes). Now here's the excellent news: everything else in life is up to you; everything else is up for grabs. You CAN make all the difference in your life. You HAVE the ability to determine what you want for yourself and what to make of your dreams. NEVER let anyone tell you otherwise. NEVER. Negative comments from other people, such as "You can't do that," "You're guaranteed to fail," or "That's impossible," are FALSE. In fact, those statements are ABSOLUTELY FALSE ... unless you believe them. I'm telling you that no matter what other people think, you CAN change anything about your current situation, you CAN improve, and most of all, you CAN succeed.

If there's no guarantee of failure, that means there is a chance of success. Any chance of a positive result is excellent—so make the most of it! I firmly believe that certain things in life are beyond our control (the weather, luck, karma). But everything else can be controlled, adjusted, and used in your favour to achieve anything you want. There are NO guarantees that you'll fail at whatever you do. There are NO guarantees you'll lose everything you own on an unwise investment. There are NO guarantees your heart will be broken in your relationship. Anything is possible. Although winning can't be guaranteed either, there are many things you can do to improve your chances of success. Everything in life is up to you. People often say that "Life is what you make of it." That statement could not be any more accurate.

<u>Anthony's True Confession No. 1:</u> ***I always try my best to be optimistic.***

I firmly believe we have the power to determine our destiny. I firmly believe our outlook, mind-set, and inner spirit can triumph over adversity. However, these three sources of power must be identified, harnessed, and properly directed to be effective. But I assure you that once you identify, harness, and properly direct your strength, it will be an undeniable force that will let you achieve your fullest potential.

This book was written for people from every possible background. My intent is to help you succeed, regardless of your circumstances. This book drives home the message that life is a wonderful thing—something to be cherished, enjoyed, and used to its fullest. But most importantly, this book is for people who want to get the most from themselves, their lives, and the lives of those around them. However, it's vital to take action—today!

The Challenge

Challenge yourself to achieve your personal success. Be your own hero. Write the next chapter of your life according to your own script. Make your dreams a reality, and most of all, find your S.M.I.L.E.

It isn't difficult to understand the steps involved in achieving success. There are three phases: Planning (Steps 1 and 2), Executing (Steps 3 and 4), and S.M.I.L.E.ing (Smiling) (Step 5). Finding your S.M.I.L.E. involves five steps:

Step 1: Getting Started
Step 2: Defining Your S.M.I.L.E.
Step 3: Managing Your Performance
Step 4: Managing Your Environment
Step 5: Once You've Found Your S.M.I.L.E.—Now What?

Phase I: Planning

Step 1: Getting Started
Step 2: Defining Your S.M.I.L.E.

These two steps help you begin your journey to success. They're extremely important steps because they involve planning, thinking, and imagining.

Phase II: Executing

Step 3: Managing Your Performance
Step 4: Managing Your Environment

These are the most challenging steps because they require you to perform, carry through, and succeed. This book will add techniques to your personal arsenal—steps you can keep at your disposal and use as you navigate the challenges that lie ahead. In addition, I have set up a website (www.AP3media.com) that will help you turn your dreams into reality. The website contains tools and articles that will help you determine your objectives, plan out a strategy, and guide you towards success.

Phase III: S.M.I.L.E.ing

Step 5: So You've Found Your S.M.I.L.E.—Now What?

This is the final step in the journey—where all the happiness is! It's where you enjoy the fruits of your labour. It's where you S.M.I.L.E. This section helps you cope with the wonderful reality that you've succeeded in your quest and achieved what you set out to do. This section will also help you decide what to do with your newfound success. Obviously, I've saved the best for last.

Are you ready?

Now, turn the page and proceed to the first phase. You must be willing to take the courageous first step. As the saying goes, "A journey of one thousand steps begins with a single step." All it takes is one step—in the right direction.

In the first phase, you will need to organize yourself, your objectives, and your emotions into a cohesive unit. This book will help you do that. The tools on the website will also help leverage your efforts.

Turn the page, and let's begin.

"If you fail to prepare, prepare to fail."

– *Author unknown*

Phase I: Planning

Introduction to Phase I

The Planning Phase involves Steps 1 (Getting Started) and 2 (Defining Your S.M.I.L.E.). I'm a hard-core planner. I adore planning. I sometimes feel I can't accomplish anything unless I plan. I learned the importance of planning at an early age, in elementary school. I would always develop an outline for my work before I set to work, especially when writing presentations, essays, and compositions. Whenever I try to improvise writing without a plan, I find myself struggling with errors, inconsistencies, and, worst of all, inefficiencies.

I firmly believe that all efficient people plan. You're a busy person. Your time is valuable. Everything moves fast these days—the Internet, e-mails, cell phones, Blackberries. There's no time to waste. There's a reason why there's such a thing as the "New York Minute" (always less than 60 seconds)—because no one in the "city that never sleeps" has the time to allocate a full minute.

Time is beyond our control. It's a valuable resource and must be used wisely. Plan your strategy before attacking. Planning is an excellent investment. Invest in time. Seeking to plan your efforts before expending them will enable you to focus your energy on what matters to you. Furthermore, you'll minimize the risk of spending time on something that's irrelevant to or inconsistent with your mission.

Planning is the first phase in your conquest of success. The first step involves getting started. The second step involves defining your S.M.I.L.E. These two steps combined constitute the planning that you need to do before you attack a given task.

Where do you start?

Only YOU can help yourself begin this journey. The techniques and strategies outlined in this book and on the website will help make it easier to start, but it all starts with you—it begins with a commitment. The beginning of any journey is the most difficult step because it involves the most effort.

Remember physics class?

We learned at school about the laws of physics, which stated that bodies at rest remain at rest and bodies in motion remain in motion. The only way to change the state of a body at rest (not moving) or a body in motion (moving) is to expend energy (effort). If you have a choice between changing your life and not changing anything at all, it would be easier to leave things unchanged.

However, if you left things unchanged, would you be any happier? I don't believe you would. If there were something you wanted to change in your life and you did nothing to change it, would you be able to live with that for the rest of your life? I simply can't accept anything that's imperfect in my life. I hope you feel the same.

Anthony's True Confession No. 2: *I am a self-confessed perfectionist.*

I firmly believe that the perfectionist bug is alive and well in all of us. I want you to discover that perfectionist trait in yourself, and nurture and develop it to serve as a driving force on your way to happiness. Not being willing to accept something just the way it is and striving for something better is a powerful motivator that can give you drive and dedication to propel you on your journey. Use it. Let this book help you get in motion.

It takes effort to change something. A body at rest can't be set in motion without effort. Do you really want to be classified as a body at rest? Wouldn't it be great to think of yourself as a body in motion, always moving in one constant direction: towards happiness and success? Do you want to settle for whatever life has handed you up to this point, or do you want more? Do you want to have your destiny dictated to you, or would you rather be free to determine your goals, develop a strategy to achieve them, and enjoy the rewards of your hard work?

If you're still reading at this point, then I believe you do want to get that little extra out of your life. There's nothing wrong with wanting more. Wanting more has both positive and negative connotations. Wanting more by being demanding of yourself (positive) is very different from wanting more by being greedy (negative). Greed is one of the seven deadly sins. Demanding more from yourself is not. You must have a desire to do better in order to succeed. You must want more in the positive sense. And you must be willing to invest the effort necessary to get your body rolling in the proper direction (body in motion).

Step 1: Getting Started (Dreams and Desire)

This is the type of soul-searching you need to do before you set out on your important journey to self-improvement, success, and happiness. Step 1 will help you start the trip. Step 1 covers the preparation involved in embarking on your mission to find your S.M.I.L.E. It's a fun step. It's all about your dreams and your desires. I prefer to start with the fun stuff to encourage everyone to begin the process. In Step 1, we discuss why dreams are the only way to start this journey. Everyone dreams, but not everyone works at making dreams a reality. How incredible would it be if your dreams were realized and came true? Would you be happy? Would you S.M.I.L.E.?

Step 1 also involves one of your most powerful emotions: desire. In this section, we discuss why desire is also a prerequisite to undertaking your journey. To be successful in finding your S.M.I.L.E., you must tap into your desire, translate it into positive energy, and use it properly. Desire is your ally, so don't hesitate to use it.

Preview of Phase II

To accomplish your goals, you must also harness, develop, and use a set of skills you already have instinctively, and use them consistently to achieve your objectives. The Performance Management strategies (Phase II) will cover how to manage your mind, body, and soul on this voyage to self-fulfillment. This book is a tool that will prove useful in managing your performance at every phase of the journey.

What is Performance Management?

Everything you're doing right now (reading this book, thinking about ways to improve your situation, planning a strategy to succeed) adds up to what I call Performance Management. To be successful and have everything you want in life, I believe you must be an expert in managing YOUR performance. Making that commitment means committing to your journey and never quitting until you succeed and you're 100% satisfied with the only result that matters: SUCCESS! Don't despair—we'll discuss Performance Management further in Phase II.

Enjoy Step 1—it's a good one.

"If you can dream it, you can do it."

– Walt Disney

Step One: Getting Started

DREAMS

Preview

- **Dreams are the first step on the path to your success.**
- **Before you can achieve success, you must dream about success.**
- **Dreams provide the vision you need to define your ultimate goal.**

Introduction

The road to your success begins with a dream. Not just any dream—***your dreams***. In order to succeed, you must dream. Dreaming lets your mind travel and explore people, places, and situations your conscious mind may not have been to yet. Dreams are fun because they are private. They are your own personal experience for you to enjoy. Here I'm not only talking about the kind of dreams you have while sleeping—I mean daydreams, too. I firmly believe that your dreams are vital to your quest to find your S.M.I.L.E.

Dreams / Daydreams

Dreams and daydreams (let's call them both "dreams" for simplicity) are important because they present the ideal. When you dream, you're thinking about what it is you want. You are visualizing your goal. You are defining your objective. I would also argue that you are clarifying your focus.

Whether you're dreaming about wealth, true love, or a better physique, one thing is clear: you're dreaming about what it is you want. I believe that you absolutely must know what you want in order to get it. It has to be clear. It has to be desirable. It must bring you pleasure. And you must really focus on it. You can't be vague about your objectives and goals at this point in the process. Ask anyone who knows me: I don't like details and details don't like me. You know the expression "the devil is in the details"? Well, this is one of the few times I believe attention to detail (your dreams) is vital. Your dream has to be clear. It must be real, so real that you can see it, touch it, taste it, and feel it. In your dream, you must be able to see yourself—it must be natural. It must be comfortable.

For example, if you're dreaming of true love, then you must be able to see that "love interest." The love interest must have personal characteristics that you see perfectly: eye colour, hair, height, weight, skin texture … everything. Your dream must come to life! You have to be able to look at your dream and make like Dr. Frankenstein, screaming "It's Alive, It's ALIVE!" If you dream that you're the greatest chef in the world, then you must be able to imagine yourself wearing a chef's hat and apron, clad all in white preparing the most mouth-watering meals. If you dream that you're an Olympic athlete, then you must picture yourself finishing first in your event and receiving the gold medal.

When you're daydreaming, make sure you have fun and let yourself go. Nobody can judge you based on your dreams. You won't lose that upcoming promotion if your dreams are too far-fetched. Do you know how many times I've imagined myself playing golf one-on-one with Tiger or rocking crowds like 50 Cent and the G Unit? True, I have no aspirations to being a professional athlete or a gangster rapper, but that doesn't stop me from having the fun of dreaming.

Dreamers

"Some men see things as they are and ask why.
Others dream things that never were and ask why not."

– *George Bernard Shaw*

I believe that special things start with a dream. I firmly believe that extraordinary people do extraordinary things based on their dreams. Martin Luther King's famous speech begins with the words: "I have a dream." Olympic athletes begin their preparations for the Olympic Games by visualizing themselves on the podium after a first-place finish, receiving the gold medal. They see themselves smiling, waving to the crowd, receiving the gold medal from the judges while their national anthem plays. I imagine it feels like the proudest moment in their life. And why not, they're only daydreaming—no one can tell them otherwise! That's what I like best about dreaming: there's no limit to what you can dream about. There are no "Dream Police" who will barge into your room, shut down your "dream operation," and place you under arrest. Your dreams are yours and yours alone. I can dream about having dinner with Halle Berry and J. Lo all I want, and no Beverly Hills court can call me a stalkerazzi (stalker / paparazzi, don't ask...) for dreaming. Daydream as vividly as possible and let your imagination be your guide.

The Ideal

Dreams should be your ideal. You have to really, really, really want what you're dreaming about. I believe that the more you want what you're dreaming about, the stronger your conviction to achieve it will be. I believe you have to want what you see in your dreams more than anything else in the world. Those are very strong words: "more than anything else in the world." If it makes you happy, why wouldn't you absolutely want it to be real? You should want it so much that Usher would call you on the phone just to say "You Got It Bad." I firmly believe that you must have a strong emotional connection to your dream. Your dream must inspire you. It must entice you. It must make you feel like you're in paradise. You must be so emotional about your dream that the thought of achieving it, in and of itself, overwhelms you. The thought of successfully realizing your dream must make you euphoric. Living your dream must make you ecstatic.

On the other hand, the thought of not having what you want in your dream must produce the opposite emotions: sadness, misery, anger. You must feel like you're missing something without the "thing" you see yourself doing or having in your dream. Right now, it would actually be helpful to feel slightly depressed about not having what you're dreaming about, but don't wallow in despair or sadness because your dream is not a reality. Feel the longing your inner self has for the dream. Embrace your innate desire—your body is telling you that it's unhappy without the ideal, it's missing something. But don't let the feelings of sadness and longing stop you. Instead, you must capitalize on your feelings of desire and make them your companion on your journey to success. You must use the feelings of desire to "will" yourself into action. It takes a spark to start the fire. Your feelings of desire for attaining your dream will be the spark that ignites the flame.

I believe that your dream must become an all-consuming obsession—something you think about morning, noon, and night. The realization that you are not currently living the way you dream about living must make your current situation feel unbearable. It must be so unbearable that your conscious mind has no choice but to heed the call to action and embark on the journey to making your dream a reality. You should feel so bad about what isn't perfect in your life that you'll stop at NOTHING to achieve perfection. The ideal in your dream must be so compelling that you feel you have no option but fulfilling your destiny by making your dream a reality.

Seventh-inning stretch:

- *You must have a dream.*
- *Your dreams represent the ideal (what you want).*
- *You must want your ideal at all costs.*
- *Realizing that you aren't living your dream must make you feel down.*
- *Never fear—the "down" feeling is temporary. It will end once you succeed—once you find your S.M.I.L.E.*
- *Let the desire for your dreams excite you.*
- *Let desire be a call to action as you begin your journey and fulfill your destiny. (We will discuss desire further in the next part of Step 1.)*

MORE ON DREAMS

Napoleon Hill: Think and Grow Rich

This book is one of my favourites. Hill refers to the imagination (what I call dreams) as the fifth step on the path toward riches (I refer to your dreams as the first step on your journey). However, Hill and I agree that you need your full creative faculties to succeed. Hill claims that "imagination must be exercised" and that "ideas are products of the imagination." I agree that you must use the creative part of your brain if you are to achieve success. We may use different terminology (dreams vs. imagination) and have different priorities (I believe that you must dream before doing anything else), but we both believe that you must dream/imagine to create the process that will culminate in finding your S.M.I.L.E.

Dr. Bob Rotella: Golf Is Not a Game of Perfect

This book makes an interesting read for golfers. It doesn't mention swing mechanics (such as hand, wrist, and elbow positions). Rotella discusses the "soft" skills golfers need, including patience, determination, vision, and focus, as well as the golfer's vision before swinging the club, which is relevant to our discussion. Rotella says that golfers must target the part of the golf course they're aiming at—specifically envisioning the next shot before setting up. Choose the part of the fairway where you want the ball to land, then target the exact spot you want the ball to stop on. The author believes that the more detailed the "vision" of the target, the better chance the golfer has of translating the shot into reality. He believes that your body will work in unison with your mind if you clearly envision the target. The target—perhaps a particular patch of grass or a leaf on the ground—must be clear, even if it's 200 or 300 yards away. The key concept is clarity, mirroring what I believe about your dreams. You need to be able to touch and feel what you see in your dreams to translate them into reality. The dream must be crystal clear so that your objective remains in your mind at all times.

Anthony, stop talking. OK, so I have a dream. What do I do now?

For now, write down your dream. Be specific. Use as much detail as possible to describe what your dream looks like. Are you dreaming you're an athlete? What sport are you playing? What team are you playing for, and in what position? Any details that will help you focus clearly on the ideal must be vividly etched in your mind.

"Whatever the mind of man can conceive and believe it can achieve."

– *Napoleon Hill*

"How do you want it?"

– *Tupac*

DESIRE

Preview:

- **You have to want your S.M.I.L.E.**
- **Desire will serve as your ignition to begin your quest.**

Introduction

Both ***dreams*** and ***desire*** are necessary at the beginning of your journey, and that's why I include them as your first step in the planning phase. Dreams help you envision the ideal. Desire is the spark—the ignition—to get you started. In addition to wanting what you're dreaming about, you must also feel that not having your S.M.I.L.E. is preventing you from achieving maximum happiness. Since there's something missing, you must take action to get it. Desire is your call to action.

Desire = Ignition and Fuel

The mere thought of considering your current reality "undesirable" may be shocking. Some may argue that not being content with your current job, current weight, or current whatever is negative. I believe it depends on your focus. When I say you should absolutely want the ideal over what you currently have, I am simply trying to give you a motivating reason to act. It takes effort to change. It takes effort to change direction, change your habits, or simply change your mind-set. If you're going to be successful, then you must ABSOLUTELY want what you don't have. The only way to do that is to create the desire for change. Let me ask you: "How bad do you want it?" Your answer will give me enough insight to measure your determination. If you answer the question without any intensity, desire, or motivation, how can you expect to achieve your goals? How can you expect to get what you want without conviction or commitment? More importantly, how do you expect to survive the challenges that lie along your path to success? Desire is passion. Use it, and use it wisely.

The benefits associated with desire are twofold. Desire serves as a spark, igniting your flame as you embark on your journey. No journey can begin without desire. Desire also provides a source of fuel and energy on your journey to success. Once you find your desire, don't let it gather dust on the shelf, like the set of encyclopaedias at my parents' house. Wear your desire like a tattoo—visible for yourself and all the world to see. People must be able to look at you and see desire burning in your eyes and in your heart. To succeed and find your S.M.I.L.E., you must become a desire machine, like the Terminator that's programmed to protect John Connor (Terminator 2 and 3). I guarantee you'll use your desire at some point in your journey. At some point, a challenge will present itself and your desire will be put to the test. Weak desire will fail. Weak desire, devoid of any passion, will crumble when challenged. Is that how you want to describe your desire? Don't you want your desire to be solid and durable? Your desire will be questioned at almost every step of your journey, so make sure it's strong and ever burning.

Leverage your desire with your dreams. Linking the two will ensure your safe passage. Your dreams represent the ideal and your desire represents the motivating force that sets you in motion. When the path gets rough, your desire will serve to remind you of your dreams. That's the link. When in doubt, go back to your dream. Remember what it was you wanted for yourself as the ideal and remind yourself of your desire for that ideal. If you can do this successfully, you will triumph over any obstacle.

Be a Tiger

Tiger Woods is the epitome of unrivalled emotion and desire. Whether he's in or out of contention in a tournament, he brings the same raw emotion (desire) with him. That emotion is what makes him so dangerous and sets him apart from the rest of the pack. Is Tiger blessed with natural talent? Yes. Does he work hard at maintaining his skills? Absolutely. Does he want to succeed at any cost? Always. You can see the fear in his opponents' eyes when he develops momentum and begins making the shots that can either bring him back into contention or cushion his lead. Unleash the tiger within yourself. You must develop the same intensity to succeed in finding your S.M.I.L.E. You're on a mission—act like it. Believe that any lack of emotion, conviction, or desire will ultimately prevent you from achieving your goals.

Seventh-inning stretch:

- *You must have desire.*
- *Desire is the ignition—it provides the spark for your journey.*
- *Desire is also an energy source to be drawn upon when necessary.*
- *Your desire will be challenged—be sure it can make the grade.*

MORE ON DESIRE

Anthony Robbins: Awaken the Giant Within

My favourite motivator, Anthony Robbins (the guy who stands 8 feet 7 inches tall, has a bigger jaw than Jay Leno, and sports a nasal voice on infomercials) examines the phenomenon of desire in his audio CD Awaken the Giant Within. Robbins uses the example of annual income tax preparation to prove the point about wanting something and motivating yourself to action. He believes in the power of decisions and firm commitment. Remember what I said earlier about having firm resolve in your desire? Robbins says that a decision without commitment is only a preference, a wish, or a weak prayer. He believes that no one can succeed without a strong commitment. Although there are certain differences in our methodology and terminology (I prefer to focus on dreams and personal desire), we both agree that you must be absolutely convinced you really want something if you are to succeed.

Robbins describes the thought process involved as the April tax deadline approaches. He points out that your initial feeling about having to complete your income tax return is dread. You hate income taxes, you don't feel like completing your tax return, and you want to put off the misery until the very last minute. However, your mind-set changes as the deadline approaches and the rapidly approaching deadline becomes your call to action. You slowly begin convincing yourself that you must complete your tax return until you want it so much that you spring to action! You've convinced yourself that the deadline must be met and requires urgent attention. You race to complete your tax return faster than a raging bull running over bystanders in Pamplona. You're focused and you don't let anything block the path to completion. You submit your tax return and settle back, knowing your mission is complete and you've earned a reprieve—till next year.

What happened between the moment you were dreading doing your taxes and the moment when you actually began to fill in your tax return? An important change occurred in your thought process. What happened was a change in desire. All of a sudden, the desire not to do the tax return was overcome by the desire to submit it before the deadline.

Desire is the spark. Your desire drives you to a change in attitude. The remarkable thing is that all this happens in your mind. Nobody tells you what to do; you simply decide that once the deadline approaches, there can be no more procrastination, no more delaying. It's time to act. You want to act. You want to meet the deadline. The thought of not being able to send your tax return in on time is undesirable. The common denominator here is desire—what you want. The stronger your desire, the better. This is why I believe it's extremely important to be clear about what you want. If your desire lacks focus or clarity, you'll find it hard to stick to. Be specific and make sure it's ABSOLUTELY what you desire. Make sure as well that what you desire is positive and will bring you pleasure (see Phase II, Step III: Your Mind).

Napoleon Hill: Think and Grow Rich

Hill also believes that desire is necessary to your quest. He tells the story of Edwin C. Barnes, a regular guy with nothing remarkable about him at all—except for his desire. Barnes wanted to go into business with the great inventor Thomas Edison. Barnes spent a considerable amount of time nurturing his desire. The idea of partnering with Edison was based not on impulse but on a desire that bordered on obsession. Hill describes in graphic detail how "Barnes' desire was not a hope, it was not a wish," but a "keen, pulsating desire, which transcended everything else. It was definite." Barnes took the train to Edison's office, introduced himself to Edison, and said that he wanted to become Edison's partner. Edison studied Barnes' appearance and manner and evaluated him (job interview). Edison apparently saw the desire in Barnes' eyes and how intent he was on working with the great inventor. Edison wrote: "He stood there before me, looking like an ordinary tramp, but there was something in the expression of his face which conveyed the impression that he was determined to get what he had come after."

When was the last time someone said the same about you and your mission to find your S.M.I.L.E.? Adopt the same conviction on your path. Edison didn't offer Barnes a partnership right away, but based on Barnes' determination, he was awarded a position in the company. Several months went by and Barnes realized that he was working for Edison, but not as a partner—he hadn't accomplished what he'd set out to do. However, with each passing day, Barnes' desire to be Edison's partner was "intensifying." Barnes' desire increased over time, up to the point when the opportunity to sell an unpopular invention created by Edison arose. Barnes rose to the occasion, no doubt a result of his ever-present desire, and successfully sold the invention. The positive results convinced Edison to make Barnes his partner. This would not have been possible without a committed, undeniable desire.

Anthony, I get it—Desire. What do I do now?

Think of adjectives to describe your desire, such as burning, committed, never-ending and so on. The adjectives will help you focus your mind on strengthening your desire. The flame of desire you have in your mind and heart couldn't be put out with a fire extinguisher. Want it at all costs. Never forget that your desire is unstoppable.

Step Two: Defining Your S.M.I.L.E.

YOUR S.M.I.L.E.

Preview

- What is your S.M.I.L.E.?
- Reader interactive section coming up...
- Fun with Internet tools from website (www.AP3media.com)

Introduction

This step is a logical progression from the work you performed in Step 1. Your quest to find your S.M.I.L.E. began with a dream and creating, nurturing, and developing your desire. Step 1 was the fun stuff. Step 2 involves the simple stuff. I want you to give your S.M.I.L.E. a name and face. It's picture-painting time, and you're the artist. I want you to formally declare (to yourself) what your S.M.I.L.E. is. You're making a sales pitch to your most important client—yourself.

Now it's time to define your objective. I'm curious: what's your definition of success? A certain amount of personal net worth? An ideal weight? An improved relationship? Do you desperately want that job promotion? What, in your opinion, constitutes success? What do you need to change or achieve in your life that will make you wake up in the morning and say to yourself: "I'm successful and I LOVE EVERYTHING about my life"?

Here again, details are vital. Be as specific about your S.M.I.L.E. as possible. Use precise language, add adjectives, mix in some verbs, to define your goals properly. Clarity is ultra-important because you will carry your objective with you on every step of the journey. There are times when the challenges will shake you up, maybe knock the wind out of you, and test your resolve. Having a clearly defined objective eliminates the guesswork. You won't have to remind yourself of your goal, since it will have been clearly documented from the beginning. That will set your brain free to do more important things, such as maintaining the appropriate level of desire, staying flexible, and being resourceful.

What do I do now, Anthony?

Several tools on the website (www.AP3media.com) were designed to accompany you on your quest: Personal Guarantee, Objective(s), Steps, and Completion Certificate. Blank copies of these documents are included after this chapter, and my personal (filled-in) copies are in Exhibit I at the end of the book.

Website Tool: Personal Guarantee

This document is a legal contract prepared by you for yourself, in which you commit to achieving your goal(s) by a specific date. Once you sign this document, there's no backing down. Obviously, you won't sue yourself for not respecting the contract, but that's beside the point. I like to have things in writing. Signatures make contracts official. In business, people promise many things. Try asking them to personally guarantee whatever it is they promise in writing and you'll notice an interesting change in attitude. In business, written contracts mean business. They are not to be taken lightly—ask any attorney.

Website Tool: Objective(s)

This document lists the single or multiple objectives you must achieve to experience true happiness. They are your S.M.I.L.E. Be clear and specific.

Website Tool: Steps

This document elaborates on the Objective(s). You list the steps that must be completed to attain each of your objectives—as many steps as necessary to provide a clear outline of what needs to be done, and in what order, to achieve your success.

Website Tool: Completion Certificate

This is the prize—patting yourself on the back for successfully completing your quest. Consider it your diploma for graduating from S.M.I.L.E. University.

The interesting twist is that you must complete this document before you can consider your journey successfully completed. In theory, the Completion Certificate should be the last step in the process. Congratulations in advance! This is what I call a visual aid, to help you focus on the finish line. It's your gold medal, to be awarded upon successful completion of the journey. BUT I want you to complete it before you start, along with the other documents. I want you to envision your success before you achieve it. You must believe you can do it. You must be convinced you'll succeed. I hope that the exercise of completing the Completion Certificate will help you with the visualization process.

Keep a printout of these tools with you at all times. Do not, I repeat, do not file the printout of these tools with your birth certificate, that picture of your high-school sweetheart, or your gym membership contract (basically, items you used at one time, but not any more). These documents will be your best friend for the next little while, so carry them with you at all times. You must never ever forget your mission. Now you have a dream and a burning desire to S.M.I.L.E., right? I want you to keep the Personal Guarantee, Objective(s), Steps and Completion Certificate with you at all times.

Use these tools—they will be extremely valuable to you on your quest!

Website Tool: Personal Guarantee

** This document is a guarantee that you will achieve your goal(s) and commit to a due date. **

Date: ______________________________

(date)

I, ____

(name)

have a personal goal: ______________________________________

____

(insert your goal)

This personal goal represents my S.M.I.L.E.

This agreement is to certify that I,

____

(name)

personally guarantee myself that I will find my S.M.I.L.E., no matter how much time, effort, and sacrifice it takes.

I will accomplish this with the help of *Finding Your S.M.I.L.E.*, www.AP3media.com, and the website tools.

I believe I will find my S.M.I.L.E. by ___________________________

(date)

I also promise that once I find my S.M.I.L.E., I will do all I can to enjoy it, take care of it, and share it with those closest to me.

Signed: ____

(signature)

Website Tool: Objectives

** This document is a list of your objective(s). **

Your S.M.I.L.E.: (S.M.I.L.E.).

Does your S.M.I.L.E. represent one or many objectives?

List your objectives:

1. (Objective 1)

2. (Objective 2)

3. (continued if necessary)

Website Tool: Steps

** This document lists the steps you will need to take to reach your objective(s). **

Your S.M.I.L.E.: (S.M.I.L.E.)

Does your S.M.I.L.E. represent one or many objectives?

List your objectives and the steps needed to achieve your objectives:

1. (Objective 1)
    a. (Step 1)

    b. (Step 2)

    c. (Step 3)

2. (Objective 2)
    d. (Step 1)

    e. (Step 2)

    f. (Step 3)

3. (Continued if necessary)

Website Tool: Completion Certificate

** This document congratulates you on successfully completing your mission and finding your S.M.I.L.E. You must complete this document BEFORE you embark on your mission. **

Date: ______________________________
(date)

This is to certify that ____
(name)

successfully found his/her S.M.I.L.E. on ____________________________
(date)

____
(name)

indicated on the Personal Guarantee that his/her S.M.I.L.E. was (S.M.I.L.E.)

This Completion Certificate is granted unconditionally to

____
(name)

in recognition of all the work, sacrifice and dedication demonstrated in finding his/her S.M.I.L.E.

CONGRATULATIONS!

Signed: ____
(signature)

"To think is easy. To act is hard. But the hardest thing in the world is to act in accordance with your thinking."

– *Goethe*

"Golf: Drive for the show, putt for the dough."

– *Author unknown*

Phase II: Executing

Introduction

I'm honoured to see that you've stuck with the program. Phase II is the most challenging phase as it includes the two most difficult steps: Managing Your Performance (Step 3) and Managing Your Environment (Step 4). You'll need all your mental, physical, and spiritual energy for this phase. This is where you earn your salary—in the execution phase. This is where you "shake your money-maker" like James Brown. This is where you take action. This phase culminates in just one result: your success—your S.M.I.L.E. Ask any golfer, even Tiger Woods, and they'll tell you that how you finish a hole (putting) is more important than how you drive the ball. Crushing 300-yard drives off the tee may be a pretty sight, but those 6-foot, 12-foot, and 18-foot putts ultimately determine whether you finish the tournament as a winner. Putting involves executing—finishing, completing what you started. Working hard at something until you achieve what you set out to do is tough work, but that's what you need to do if you want to win.

Don't let the fact that this is the most challenging phase discourage you—it's also the most rewarding, because it lets you learn things about yourself you probably never knew before. You'll discover previously hidden potential, skills, and talents. Perhaps the best thing about this phase is that it's the continuation of what you began in Phase I. This is where you add effort, mix in some dreams, and add a lot of desire for the purpose of fulfilling your destiny—finding your S.M.I.L.E. How great is it to know that by the end of this phase, your dream will have become a reality and your S.M.I.L.E. will be real?

Performance Management Revisited

Phase II is where you earn your keep and become the master of your S.M.I.L.E. domain. But you must also become your own Performance Manager. How you manage your performance will ultimately determine your success. If finding your S.M.I.L.E. is the objective, Performance Management is the vehicle that propels you to your objective. Performance Management is the main theme of Steps 3 and 4. You must constantly monitor your performance as you go through the process. If you don't analyze your progress, you could be unaware of inefficiencies, issues, or other important matters. Pay attention to yourself as you travel towards your goal. You need to be in top physical and mental shape for the journey. To achieve optimum results, use the techniques outlined in Phase II to manage your performance.

Step 3: Managing Your Performance

The third and fourth steps involve acting as your own performance manager and managing both your mind and your body. You must believe that "success comes from within." It starts with you, and it starts right now. Don't wait for favourable conditions like a good hair day, after your summer vacation, or the end of the school term. Drop everything else and take action now. The only person who can get your S.M.I.L.E. project up and running is you. Yes, others will come into play in Step 4; however, you are still and always will be the person responsible for your success. You are the star of the movie S.M.I.L.E. You are the CEO of Finding Your S.M.I.L.E. Enterprises and the author of your own success. This phase of the journey starts with you. And you must take this responsibility very seriously.

Temporary Obstacles: Introduction

What if you encounter obstacles along your path? How do you deal with them? How do you react? Are there ways to prepare for obstacles? These are valid and extremely important questions. Chances are you will encounter obstacles along your path, as I have—many challenges, hurdles, and failures. Sometimes it feels as though every step forward leads to a difficult situation or an issue that must be dealt with before you can move on to the next step. Sometimes it may feel as though the challenges are just waiting to pounce on you like a lion on unsuspecting prey. I believe this is normal. Life is full of unexpected events, and it's crazy to assume that everything will remain as it is. To expect success to simply present itself at your front door without having to strive for it is bananas … b-a-n-a-n-a-s.

In Phase II, I will discuss, analyze, and dissect the most significant temporary obstacle you may encounter on your journey to success: **fear**. I say "temporary obstacle" because fear is simply temporary (it won't last long). I believe there's no such thing as a permanent obstacle—only temporary obstacles. There's no such thing as an insurmountable challenge—only surmountable challenges you must triumph over on your path to victory. Do you see the difference? By using adjectives that minimize the importance of pejorative nouns (temporary obstacles, surmountable challenges), you subconsciously program yourself to interpret challenges, setbacks, and obstacles as temporary. Are they really? That depends on the strength of your resolve and your will. When you encounter the hurdles you must leap over in order to achieve success and you convince yourself they are short-term and you will ultimately succeed, nothing can stop you! Use adjectives to downplay the importance of challenges on your path to your S.M.I.L.E. Use them often. They're cheap and plentiful. We'll come back to adjectives in the Performance Management: Strategies section.

You must be ready for any temporary hurdle (challenge) at any given moment. Nothing can stand in your way unless you let it. You alone control the size, nature, and potential impact of an obstacle. If an obstacle presents itself and you are able to manage your mind, body, and emotions, then the hurdle is temporary—it's present until you dispel it (get rid of it). If you're unable to surmount an obstacle, then it becomes a permanent barrier that prevents you from reaching your full potential. MAKE HURDLES TEMPORARY. You can rise to any challenge and defeat any opponent. What matters is your state of mind and body. Don't let obstacles stand in the way of your dreams.

In the next section, I discuss various strategies for dealing with your temporary hurdles. Picture yourself as an Olympic athlete, jumping over hurdle after hurdle on your way to the finish line. I believe that any challenge is surmountable with the proper tools.

Prove to yourself, your friends and family that you truly are unstoppable by clearing any hurdles in your way. You will be able to leap over some hurdles easily while others will take a little more effort—but your objective should be to leap over all of them. The end result is what counts and whether you defeat your temporary obstacles quickly or after a prolonged period of time is of no consequence. The point is to make sure the obstacles are temporary.

Strategies: Introduction

Phase II presents various techniques that will help you with Performance Management—important strategies that will help you achieve your wildest dreams. I hope that these strategies will inspire you to reach your fullest potential and find your S.M.I.L.E.

Step 4: Managing Your Environment

You must also manage your environment successfully to achieve your maximum potential. Your environment consists of family, friends, and other people you encounter on your path to success. How you manage your performance with others will also determine your success. One of my favourite lines from the film Jerry Maguire is when Jay Moore says: "It's not show friends, it's show business"—meaning that Jerry should forget friendship and focus on his own self-interest. I partially agree with that statement. Yes, your S.M.I.L.E. is your business. You must make it your own, but don't discount the benefits of getting those around you involved in your S.M.I.L.E. operation. You'll need friends to get through and find your S.M.I.L.E., but I strongly suggest you save them for Step 4 (after you complete Step 3).

Good luck with Phase II: Executing!

"People are like stained-glass windows.
They sparkle and shine when the sun is out, but when
the darkness sets in, their true beauty is revealed
only if there is a light from within."

– Elisabeth Kübler-Ross

Step Three: Managing Your Performance

YOUR MIND

Preview

- **Your journey begins with your mind.**
- **To successfully find your S.M.I.L.E., you must first manage your mind.**
- **There are three aspects of your mind that must be managed: *perception, attitude, and mentality***

Introduction

The mind is an incredible thing. It is often said that we use only 10% of our minds, which astonishes me—who knows what we could achieve if we used all of our mental faculties? Your mind is the single most incredible instrument you're equipped with—a computer that's responsible for memory, creativity, and intelligence. Have you ever marvelled at the incredible complexity and power of the human mind? Your mind keeps moving every minute of every day. Keep in mind, however, as Uncle Ben tells Peter Parker in Spider-Man, "With great power comes great responsibility." Your mind is more powerful than any super-computer on the face of the earth. It's so powerful that you can achieve many great things once your mind's power is properly harnessed. Unfortunately, the mind may also be tainted by bad habits and problems such as addiction. You were born with this wonderful resource, and it's your responsibility to cherish it, nourish it, and use it wisely.

You must have a fully present mind to complete your journey and find your S.M.I.L.E. You cannot complete the journey without it. In particular, I believe the following components of your mind are crucial on your quest: **perception, attitude, and mentality**. These three factors form the mental building blocks you need to succeed.

Perception

Perception of yourself and your goal are one important aspect of managing the performance of your mind. How you perceive yourself will have a major impact on your performance. How you perceive your goal also has a major impact. These perceptions must be managed to ensure peak performance. You must be a Performance Manager.

Perception of Your Goals

Your desire is extremely important. As I asked you in the previous section, "How bad do you want your S.M.I.L.E."? You must want whatever it is you're dreaming about more than anything in the world, and feel that you want to fulfill your dream immediately because you want it so bad. This is your perception of your goal—you perceive it to be ABSOLUTELY NECESSARY. You must have a burning desire to succeed. You must feel passionate about your goal, and perceive it as something you simply can't do without.

"To succeed … you need to find something to hold on to,
something to motivate you, something to inspire you."

– *Tony Dorsett*

If your desire for your goal is weak, then perhaps your goal isn't worthy of all the effort. Your goal must represent your future happiness. You have to want it for yourself because you want to have it. Have you ever done something for someone else half-heartedly? Have you ever been forced or obliged to do something you really didn't want to do? Wasn't it torture? Imagine yourself working somewhere that doesn't satisfy you or your career aspirations. Doesn't your workday feel endless? Don't you feel mentally exhausted at the end of your shift? It feels like torture because you don't value it. When you're working towards something you're not passionate about, your energy level drops, your mood darkens, your limbs feel like blocks of cement—basically, it doesn't feel good. This is life without passion or desire.

Unfortunately, in the short term, we sometimes have to do things we don't want to do (such as working in a job we don't like) for other reasons—needing money to pay the bills, needing to be patient until the next promotion, or needing to make our parents happy.

Did you notice the change in terminology? When I describe your S.M.I.L.E., I use words like "desire," "passion," and "wanting it bad." When I describe things you aren't passionate about, I use the word "need," as in "need to do this..." or "need to do that..." This is lack of desire. Needing to do something is about as much fun as a trip to the dentist. That's why I'm so vocal about you wanting your goal. Don't feel as though you "need" to find your S.M.I.L.E., because then it falls into the same category as "needing to go on a diet" or "needing to start exercising," or "needing to start saving money." Boring. Your quest for your S.M.I.L.E. has to be intense enough to keep you up at night and make you want to jump out of bed in the morning and mount an attack to achieve some progress towards your goal. Proper perception of your goals is key. Make yourself want your goal. The stronger the emotions you feel about your goals, the more effective your efforts to achieve success will be.

It's difficult to motivate yourself by wanting something because you "need" it. Let's take quitting a bad habit as an example. Nearly everyone has struggled to overcome a weight problem, some form of addiction, or another negative situation. We're all human and we all have our challenges. However, if you hope to succeed, you must want to change more than anything in the world.

Many friends and family members have confided in me that they also struggle to control their weight and break the cycle of overeating. This is a challenge many people have to face, including me.

Anthony's True Confession No. 3: ***I have a habit of overeating junk food.***

I have an addiction to snack foods like soft drinks and potato chips. I can sympathize with others who face the same challenge and struggle with it every day. When I used to binge on junk food I noticed several things about myself. If you suffer from overeating, tell me if this pattern sounds familiar.

I noticed that: 1) I would eat too much junk food; 2) my self-control disappeared when I was feeling weak or bored; and 3) overeating junk food was unhealthy and made me feel down. But the flaws in my reasoning can be

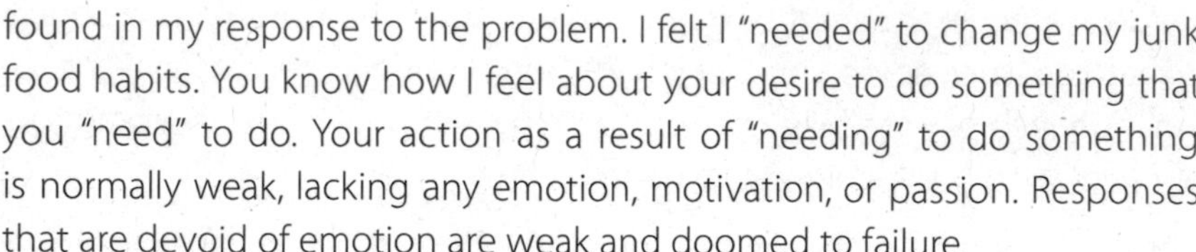

found in my response to the problem. I felt I "needed" to change my junk food habits. You know how I feel about your desire to do something that you "need" to do. Your action as a result of "needing" to do something is normally weak, lacking any emotion, motivation, or passion. Responses that are devoid of emotion are weak and doomed to failure.

My resolve to eat less junk food never had a chance! I kept telling myself: "Anthony, you need to avoid junk food. You need to eat less junk food. You need to start exercising." Forget it. I could have repeated those thoughts to myself from morning to night without getting any closer to my goal. I wasn't passionate about changing. I didn't perceive my goal with desire. I didn't want it at all costs. If someone had asked me, "Anthony, how bad do you want it?" I wouldn't honestly have been able to say, "More than anything in the world." And that was the problem—no passion. No desire. My goal perception didn't motivate me enough to act.

If you hope to change your goal perception, you have to inject some emotion into the mix. I can hear you ask: "Anthony, how do I create passion?" "How can you boost your desire for your objectives while avoiding the need-to-do-something syndrome?" Excellent question. Harness your mind on your journey. If you can't quit junk food, what are you telling yourself? You know it's bad for you in the long term, but you're saying that the buzz from eating junk food in that moment is more pleasurable than the buzz from being fit and maintaining long-term health. That scary thought is consistent with most addictions—the sacrifice of long-term benefits for short-term gains at any cost. The trick here is to change your perception and program your mind in a different direction—which is simple in theory, but challenging in practice. You have to want to change. You have to desire a change from your current mind-set that says, "I will continue eating junk food because it gives me short-term pleasure." Instead, you have to program yourself to think that junk food is undesirable and your long-term health is more important (perception).

In my case, there was some desire for change (cutting down on junk food), but not enough to qualify as true desire. I was associating pleasure with junk food. That association had to be changed before I could reduce my junk food intake. You must destabilize the old thought pattern (junk food=pleasure) with a new thought pattern (health=pleasure; junk food=unhappiness).

The thought of junk food had to revolt me—make me sick to my stomach, so sick that I couldn't even imagine myself wanting to eat it any more.

Once you accomplish this, your perception of the goal has changed. All of a sudden, the long-term health issue has suddenly moved up in importance. Imagine the power of a shift in mental perception or goal perception. If you can foster feelings of disgust for junk food, then it becomes that much simpler to foster positive emotions about the alternative—a healthy lifestyle. If you can successfully program your mind to remember the way junk food makes you feel after eating it, then it will associate that same bad feeling with junk food in the near future as well. Now, every time you're offered junk food, you'll hesitate before eating it. And it's exactly that hesitation you want when you're trying to destabilize a bad habit. I believe that if you can halt the progress of a bad habit, you can eventually conquer it.

Stories about addiction break my heart. Addictions are brutal, for the addict and for his or her friends, family, and colleagues. The most common addictions involve smoking, eating, and gambling. A close friend of mine was once a heavy smoker. He would claim that he enjoyed smoking and could stop at any time—therefore, he said, he was not addicted to cigarettes. However, after a while, I noticed my friend singing a different tune. He'd tell me how he was starting to crave cigarettes more and more. Eventually, what he perceived as an innocent pastime became a full-blown addiction. He was hooked on cigarettes, a slave to the addiction. My buddy tried to quit smoking in many different ways—abstaining ("cold turkey"), nicotine gum, and hypnotism (it's true!). Today, I'm proud to say he's beaten the addiction, though he does relapse from time to time. He'll sneak in a cigarette between drinks at a party or smoke a cigar after a big meal. The habit obviously remains, but he probably smokes only 1 to 5 percent as much as he did at the peak of his addiction.

I've never been to an Alcoholics Anonymous or Narcotics Anonymous meeting, but I've heard that AA and NA encourage participants to give their first name only, which promotes anonymity ("Hello, my name is John...") and admit to being an addict ("...and I am an alcoholic...").

This is significant. Forget about who you are; if you are ready to get help, you must admit you have a problem—admit your weakness. Admit that your current situation is problematic and undesirable. You can't get help managing your addiction if you don't perceive the addiction to be a problem. If you can admit that you're doing something that's bad for you (overeating, smoking, abusing substances), then you've taken the first step towards seeking help because you are developing your desire for a change. I assume that if you know you're doing something that's bad for you, you'll want to pinpoint what you can do to turn it around and make it positive. You have to admit to yourself that your current actions are not appropriate and your current behaviour is not pleasurable. Perhaps the addiction provides temporary relief from pressure at work, a nagging spouse, or some other stressful situation, but you realize that you're harming yourself and those around you.

My friend initially claimed that he liked smoking and associated pleasure with his habit. However, as time went on and his health deteriorated, he began to see a different side of his addiction—the ugly side. He told me that he would often have a brutal cough that persisted for hours, and feel his lungs, stamina, and general mood worsening. The negative consequences of the addiction were becoming even more frequent. However, my friend continued smoking because he was addicted and did not possess the resolve (desire for change) to quit. He wasn't yet fed up with coughing and feeling crappy. Slowly, I watched him develop an utter disgust for smoking. He was associating less pleasure with smoking and more with wanting to feel good and healthy (change in perception). Eventually, he fostered his disgust for smoking by smoking more—albeit at odd times.

This may sound counter-intuitive. In the beginning, my buddy smoked when he wanted to and found it pleasurable. However, as time passed and the harmful side effects appeared, the pleasurable aspects of smoking were called into question. All previous attempts to quit smoking (abstinence, nicotine gum, and hypnotism) had failed because he perceived cigarettes as being "pleasurable," believed that he "needed" to quit, and perceived cigarettes as being harmful, but not harmful enough to drop everything and stop smoking.

My friend solved his perception problem by convincing himself that smoking was not pleasurable. He began smoking more, but at odd times. He would smoke before meals, instead of afterwards, which spoiled his appetite and the taste of his meal. He'd smoke at work, which he'd never done before, reducing his productivity. And he'd smoke when he didn't have a craving, which is unpleasant. Smoking was now getting in the way of other activities, such as eating, working, and enjoying life, while continuing to damage his health. Smoking was no longer pleasurable, and it seemed that quitting smoking would give him more pleasure than continuing to smoke.

His perception had shifted. He wanted to get cigarettes and cigars out of his life—they were disgusting. In the end, he succeeded in battling his addiction. He told me he remembers smoking his last cigarette as being the most disgusting thing he'd ever done. What a difference from a few years before, when my buddy would need a smoke before doing anything!

Compare this with an acquaintance who also stopped smoking cigarettes, but says he remembers his last cigarette fondly (!) and enjoyed every cigarette he ever smoked up until the very last one before he quit (!). Who do you think has the greater chance of a relapse, my buddy who claims the occasional cigarette still disgusts him or my acquaintance who also quit smoking, but still sees cigarettes as a source of pleasure? If you don't want to quit, no one can help you. And the way to quit is to be so totally fed up with the addiction that it makes you sick just thinking about it.

Forget about "needing" to change, you have to want to change. You have to want the long-term benefits more than the short-term satisfaction that comes with a cost. But if you aren't passionate about changing, the process will fail you and you'll revert to the bad thought patterns.

How you perceive your goals is crucial. How do you feel about your goals? Do you feel you "need" to achieve your goals because you have bills to pay or need to make your mother happy? Or do you see your goal as holding long-term satisfaction for you? Program your mind, and witness the incredible results once you have your goal perception properly aligned.

Attitude

Attitude is another important part of your mind-set—the second mental faculty you must manage on your path to finding your S.M.I.L.E.

"It is not your aptitude, but your attitude that determines your altitude."

– Zig Ziglar

I'm certain Ziglar didn't mean to say that aptitude is irrelevant, because I believe you do need some skill and talent to succeed. But note that he says attitude has a major impact on your success (altitude). I firmly believe that you must have a positive attitude in order to succeed. I have never heard of anyone with a negative mind-set finding meaningful long-term happiness, because their negativity overshadows the joys of success.

"The key to success is not through achievement, but through enthusiasm."

– Malcolm Forbes

Negativity is like cancer. Negativity darkens your thoughts, clouds your focus, and poisons your heart. Negativity will only hamper your efforts and can't possibly help you along on your journey.

Anthony's Real-Life Example: Perception and Attitude

Setback: ***negative attitude; anxiety about entering university***

Lesson learned: ***the importance of optimism***

Throughout my university and post-graduate years, I never changed my perception of my objective to graduate successfully. I knew I wanted it. My dream was to become a Chartered Accountant. My desire was definite—I was prepared to sacrifice anything, including my social life, my activities, and my hairline, to fulfill my dream. Obtaining my Canadian Chartered Accounting designation was my S.M.I.L.E., my clearly defined objective, and the answer to my dreams.

The challenging journey ahead, however, would mean at least seven years of post-secondary studies (1996–2003). I had to make a personal commitment to that journey at the age of 19, when a guy's priorities include video games, the NFL, and impressing the ladies. No one in my family demanded that I choose this direction—I truly wanted it for myself; I perceived the goal as being highly desirable.

My attitude, however, left a great deal to be desired. I had developed a poor attitude after completing my two years of post-secondary studies (Quebec students complete two years of "college"—a bridge between high school and university). With hindsight, I attribute my negativity/anxiety to the fact that I was starting university. My college years (1994–1996) had been amazing. I'd hung out with many of the same best friends I have today. Parties, fun, and social events (video game tournaments, poker tournaments, club parties) were plentiful, and we were always laughing. Who'd want to leave all that?

However, as the eldest of my friends, I was the first to leave for university. I wasn't frightened—I knew I wanted to graduate and I knew I could do it. But I knew that from that moment on, I would never again be in a classroom with my 10 closest buddies every day. And so I was extremely negative about the next part of the journey (university).

I remember the day when a thick package arrived at my house—my acceptance package from McGill. My buddy and my parents were ecstatic, and urged me to open it right away. My joys and anxieties were confirmed—I had been accepted into the accounting program. While my buddy was busy popping champagne corks with my parents, I was feeling mixed emotions. I was extremely happy because the acceptance was another successfully completed step on my journey to finding my S.M.I.L.E. However, I knew that my more challenging university years were coming soon to a theatre near me, as it was just a few weeks before the start of the semester. And that letter marked the official end of my college years. Now I had to curtail my social activities and devote all my energies to academics—which I knew very well did not include video games, club parties, or hanging out with my buddies from morning until night. I would have to start acting like an adult—the horror!

The day my acceptance letter arrived marked the beginning of a negative attitude I unfortunately maintained throughout my five-year university career (including graduate studies), from which I did not emerge for several years. Luckily, I changed my attitude after successive failures. That change finally gave me the desire to pass the Chartered Accountant exam and make my S.M.I.L.E. a reality.

A few words here about the harm of adopting a negative attitude. It is extremely important that you use the insights in this section to make sure you take a positive attitude to boost your chances of finding your S.M.I.L.E.

Negativity is poison. The danger is that you may not be aware of the poison in your system until it's too late and you suffer a debilitating loss. Negativity is a silent killer—it may not announce its arrival, but there's no mistaking its harmful effects. Negativity distracts you and causes you to focus on the bad instead of the good. If a poor attitude makes you see only the bad in your life, how can you expect to enjoy the good and positive things once they do arrive?

Positivity and negativity are born of habits and repetition. If you're a pessimist, you won't be able to "switch" overnight once the good things start coming your way. Worse still, you may not even see the bright side of things once they arrive because you aren't looking for them. If you're an optimist and always make light of negative events and cherish life's joyous events, you have the best attitude for finding your S.M.I.L.E.

I was feeling resentful because I knew I'd have to make new friends and hang out with other people besides my crew of buddies. I saw university as a necessary evil. I was going to have to struggle with studying, completing assignments, and writing gruelling exams. I had a horrible attitude.

With hindsight, as I tell my sister all the time now that she's at university, it was a truly incredible experience. I regret that I didn't get everything I could out of university. I regret not having joined a fraternity, any social committees, or the student council. Luckily, I did enjoy meeting different students from various backgrounds, many of whom I've had the pleasure of working with since then in my professional career.

That first day at McGill should have alerted me to my poor attitude and negative impression of university. I met an old friend from high school on the bus that day who was attending the same university and taking the same classes. He in turn introduced me to a group of four others who became our informal study group of friends throughout my undergraduate program. How lucky I was to have such a great time my first day of university! But I couldn't see it at the time.

A negative attitude is a horrible liability. Adopt a positive attitude on your journey to fulfilling your destiny and finding your S.M.I.L.E.—it will make the trip all the more enjoyable!

Mentality

The final aspect of your mind that you must manage as a Performance Manager is your mentality. To find your S.M.I.L.E., you must adopt a winning mentality. I believe the mentality that's so vital to making your dreams a reality includes hard work, commitment, and humility in equal measure.

Like it or not, it will take hard work to succeed. Hard work doesn't necessarily mean physical work. The mental preparation (reading books, planning, and thinking) you invest in your project also counts as work. Don't think your S.M.I.L.E. will be easy to find. But don't get discouraged—you're already taking the right steps to prepare yourself. Reading this book is an excellent first step. I also suggest that you read books by Robert Kiyosaki (Rich Dad Poor Dad) and Napoleon Hill (Think and Grow Rich) and listen to audio CDs from Anthony Robbins. Also check out the other books I mention here, and any other sources of inspiration your friends and family may recommend.

Accept the fact that you'll have to make an effort to succeed. Some people still believe they can achieve their dreams without any effort or sacrifice. Perhaps it's possible to succeed without working, and perhaps you know someone who "made it" the easy way, but I don't believe you can get everything you want consistently without hard work.

> "After years of failed get-rich-quick schemes, I know
> I will get rich with this scheme and quick."
>
> *– Homer Simpson*

To get what you want, I believe you must give something up. To get into shape, you have to exercise regularly and maintain a healthy diet. To buy a nice car, you have to save up. The natural temptation, of course, is to choose the shortcut or the easy way out. It takes hard work to get anywhere, unless you happen to be a rich kid who's inherited a fortune or a lucky guy who's won the lottery.

Ask any professional athlete about their daily routine and you'll find out just how much preparation time goes into playing their favourite sports. CEOs of Fortune 500 companies will gladly tell you how they struggled, learned, and devoted all their time and energy to their career to make it to the top. Ask them what it takes to keep their position and they'll tell you that it's even more hard work, because the world is extremely competitive and anyone who's not willing to invest their time and energy won't make it very far.

Robert Kiyosaki, author of the Rich Dad Poor Dad series, notes how necessary it is to be willing to "pay the price" if you hope to gain financial freedom. Everything in life has a price tag, and it's up to us to determine what that price is and pay it. Kiyosaki explains how to find financial freedom and become financially self-sufficient. He firmly believes that in order to become rich, you must own or invest in a business—skills that can't be developed overnight. Kiyosaki suggests ways to develop your financial skills, such as finding a mentor, reading books, taking courses, volunteering, and experimenting with projects to encourage learning by trial and error. He says it still amazes him how many people ask him what it takes to create wealth, and after he tells them the price (investing in your financial education), many seek other opinions or think it sounds too hard. Of course it's difficult—if it were easy, we'd all be wealthy!

Remember Physics 101? It takes effort to set a body in motion. Develop your mind and accept that fact. I believe it's healthier to convince yourself that hard work and effort are required than to fool yourself by thinking it will be easy to succeed.

Anthony's Real-Life Example: Hard Work

Setback: ***repeating courses at McGill; history repeating itself at Concordia***
Lessons learned: ***perseverance, hard work, humility***

I made all the necessary sacrifices throughout my undergraduate career in the Bachelor of Accounting program at McGill. I knew it would take hard work to compete with the best and brightest students in the program, and

I'd need top marks to gain admission to the graduate program. I attended most of my classes and spent hours studying at the library and at home. And I summoned my courage and swallowed my pride when I had to repeat the courses I'd failed before I could obtain my degree.

It broke my heart to tell my friends I couldn't go out with them. I knew I had to complete my assignments and study for exams to have any hope of succeeding. It took an extra summer to graduate from McGill, but I did it. The undergraduate Bachelor of Commerce program was a prerequisite for entering graduate school and making it all the way to the final accounting exam that would grant me my practitioner's license and accounting designation. The years I spent at McGill (1996–1999) qualify as the most gruelling years of my life, but they were worth the effort, and I'd do it again with a smile if I had to.

On to Concordia...

In 1999, I entered a postgraduate program at Concordia that would lead to the Chartered Accounting exam. That meant completing postgraduate accounting courses, passing the "mock exam" offered in the summer prior to the exam, and passing the exam offered once a year in September.

I assumed the graduate program couldn't possibly be more difficult, exhausting, and strenuous than my undergraduate years. Wrong, yet again. Concordia was brutal. Nearly all the students in the program were articling in accounting firms by day and taking night courses. My brain is mush after dinner, so night courses severely tested my natural body clock. With day jobs to manage, we were competing at work and school for the same goal: to graduate from the program and take the examination (which is similar to the bar exam for lawyers). The courses were interesting, and I learned a lot from both my academic and work experience throughout my years of articling.

We were a competitive bunch, always striving for the best. There was a great deal of pressure. Nervous and eating anything I could get my hands on, I gained a solid 10 to 15 pounds.

I failed my share of graduate classes as well, struggling to complete extra courses and watch my colleagues advance while I was held back. By taking most of the extra classes on my own time, I was able to arrive at the final summer preparatory program prior to graduating from Concordia (this is still prior to the final exam) with my colleagues, but it was very hard work. All I had left to do was complete the summer prep program (which included a mock exam similar to the one I'd have to write in the fall to earn my accounting designation).

In life, there is the easy way, the difficult way, and the extremely difficult way to succeed. Most of my colleagues seemed to take the easy way—I don't remember many of them having to repeat as many courses as I did to get to that final summer program. I chose the extremely difficult route to success. I was one of the few who didn't make it out of the final summer program in 2001. My buddies went on to the exam while I went back to work and fielded questions about my recent failure. It felt horribly embarrassing to come to the final step in my graduate studies and fail. Now I'd have to wait until the next summer to re-take the summer prep program, pass it, and take the exam. The accounting profession in Montreal is a very small community. I came to be known in my group of friends as the guy who failed—a title I'd hold, not with pride, until the next summer. I was learning a lot about humility.

The next summer (2002) finally arrived and I had the pleasure of taking the summer prep program alongside my then girlfriend, whom I later married. (Yes, we're both Chartered Accountants. No, we don't work together. No, we don't talk about work all day. I just felt the need to get that cleared up before proceeding.) My wife is one year younger than I am, so you can imagine how thrilled I was to be in the same class as her. Luckily, our hard work, efforts, and sacrifices (which were second nature by that point) paid off for both of us and we both completed the summer prep program and became successful graduate students. We could now write the exam in September, after about two months of full-time self-directed study. With hindsight, my graduate experience was even more difficult than my undergraduate program. I automatically assumed the worst was over and that I should be able to coast to the exam on cruise control, succeed, and become a Chartered Accountant. I was proven wrong—yet again.

The summer of 2002 was one of the best summers of my life (apart from the fact that Italy's national team was bounced from the FIFA World Cup on questionable officiating—six disallowed goals and a send-off to the captain in the quarter-final game, I think not…). The self-study was fun and I remember the time vividly.

The exam, a three-day affair in September, was the most exhausting, stressful, energy-consuming experience I'd ever been through. The huge hall held 1,000 candidates. I couldn't even see the students on the other side of the room. We'd heard horror stories of students collapsing and crying in the exam room. The exam was difficult yet fair, and our brains were fried for several days. We anxiously awaited the announcement of the results in December. My wife passed, but I failed. I was ecstatic for her, but disappointed and upset at the turn of events.

Everyone around me feared I'd drop out and abandon my dream, but I had other plans. I'm one of those people who must constantly battle for survival. Nothing comes easy for me. Throughout college and university, I would get lower marks than my peers and could never understand why. I always felt I had to work harder than everyone else to survive. Luckily, this adversity throughout my academic career helped me develop the right mentality for dealing with disappointment. I was so used to struggling that I wasn't surprised at having to study for the exam a second time while most of the students I knew had successfully passed. Since I had the proper mentality, the decision to re-take the exam the following summer was simple.

Of course, there were consequences to that decision. It would mean taking six months off from work (lost salary), with absolutely no guarantee of success (the exam format changed in 2003, so I had no edge over a first-time writer), and I'd have to endure the stigma of attempting the exam once more and risking another failure. People treat you differently, as if you're inadequate, when you fail.

I decided to re-take the exam in 2003 and informed my parents, friends, and employer of my decision. I knew it was what I wanted to do. I'm accustomed to challenges and dealing with adversity. I completed the exam and was ecstatic to learn that I'd successfully obtained the Chartered Accounting designation and could now be counted among the elite professionals in the industry.

Conclusion: Your Mind

My story had a happy ending, but I did have to endure a significant amount of hardship over my academic career. I always knew what direction I wanted to take (perception). The decision to re-take the exam in 2003 was simple, because I had a concrete desire: to be a Chartered Accountant. There was no other career for me. I was lacking in the attitude department since I looked at my path negatively. That certainly made my journey no easier and prevented me from experiencing all the other joys of university. Luckily, I had the winning mentality that compensated for my shortfalls. I knew there was no easy way to accomplish my goals and it would take sacrifice, determination, and hard work to succeed.

Always remember the three components to your mind: ***perception, attitude, and mentality***.

Next Step: Your Body

In the next chapter, we'll discuss the importance of managing your body—the second important aspect of performance management. And we'll look at the two most critical "temporary" obstacles: **fear and risk**, as well as how to manage the performance of mind and body and develop strategies that will help you combat fear and risk.

"I finally realized that being grateful to my body was key to giving more love to myself."

– Oprah Winfrey

YOUR BODY

Preview

- **Your journey begins with your mind and continues with your body.**
- **To successfully find your S.M.I.L.E., you must first manage your mind and then your body.**

Introduction

Mankind has always had a fascination with the human body. From Michelangelo's David to Eva Longoria, a beautiful body is something we all can admire and appreciate. Your body is the pillar (support) for your mind. Never underestimate the role your body plays in your quest to find your S.M.I.L.E.

Although your mental health will be of primary importance in your quest, your physical health comes a close second. Your mind directs, your body follows. However, as with yin and yang, your mind needs your body, since no one can succeed with mental capacity alone. Proper mental and physical health is crucial to your journey to success.

Your Body: The Details

Your body serves as the main pillar for your mind. Mental health encompasses your perception, attitude, and mentality. Physical health means being strong and energetic.

Energy

It will take loads of physical energy to succeed in your mission. Make sure that your energy level is at its peak to sustain the wear and tear it will take to find your S.M.I.L.E. Keep that energy fuel tank topped up at all times. Maintaining the right energy level will give you the strength and bravado to challenge the potential temporary obstacles in your path through a constant, sustained effort—the very definition of persistence. Any successful person will tell you how much they value the qualities of energy, persistence, and sustained effort as they proceed towards achieving their goals in life.

Let's take a savings plan as an example. Financial experts agree that it's important to save money regularly—preferably by setting aside a regular amount on a regular basis, such as every week or every month. Make good habits part of your everyday routine. Making small, regular contributions to a savings plan may not seem like much at the time, but the cumulative effects over the months, years, and decades can be quite impressive. Never underestimate the value of energy and persistence.

Persistence means delivering sustained efforts to achieving the same purpose in a constant and focused manner. It takes energy to do this, so be sure to monitor your energy levels in your quest for success. See the Strategies section of Phase II for tips on keeping your energy level high.

Strength

Strength and energy are closely related. Energy determines the persistence/sustainability of your efforts to succeed, while strength determines how effective your efforts will be. Strength has many facets: physical, emotional, and/or inner strength. You need all the components of strength to survive your journey. You will encounter many temporary obstacles along the way, and you must have the courage, energy, and strength to face them or risk not succeeding. Different circumstances require different forms of strength. Temporary obstacles that cause anxiety/fear will summon your inner strength and courage. Other challenges that require a significant work effort will oblige you to rely on your physical strength—an invaluable ally on your journey.

<u>Anthony's Real-Life Example:</u> Energy and Strength

Setback: ***limited energy, especially for night courses; panic attacks; nausea***
Lessons learned: ***pacing; keeping up my energy level and stamina; surmounting a string of disappointments***

Finding my S.M.I.L.E. on graduation and then obtaining my Chartered Accounting designation pushed both my mind and my body to the limit. My body faced many challenges on my journey to my S.M.I.L.E.

The path to becoming a Chartered Accountant was riddled with temporary obstacles. Three-hour night courses had to be taken after articling in accounting firms during the day. The work during the day alone would be enough for the average person—challenging, demanding, and consuming. An evening course load plus required study-time on the weekends added up to a bountiful bonanza of back-breaking work. We were all well aware, however, that this was what it would take to become a Chartered Accountant in Quebec. It took all my energy to handle daytime work, evening, courses, and weekend study sessions. That's why I believe it's so important to marshal all your energy for the challenges that await you in finding your S.M.I.L.E.

<u>Anthony's True Confession No. 4:</u> ***I'm not very strong physically.***

I suffer from migraines. If I pull an "all-nighter," I have to sleep for the next two days. A strong physical specimen I'm not, but I try my best all the same.

On top of the gruelling day, night, and weekend hours, we had to endure three-hour midterms and four-hour finals (final exams normally accounted for 75% to 100% of our grade). The finals were enormously stressful, as we knew that the entire semester hinged on our performance in that examination room that evening. Luckily, my body grew accustomed to the rigid schedule of daytime work and evening studies despite my frequent migraines.

I failed several classes in my three years of post-graduate studies at Concordia University, and the physical toll of re-taking those classes was enormous. I'm not fond of sitting in class or studying, so failing classes and being forced to endure re-takes was mental torture, but that was the personal price I would have to pay if I wanted to succeed.

In 2001, I finally made it to the last summer course I needed to pass to graduate from Concordia and be admitted to write the exam in September. The course culminated with a mock final exam, similar to the September exam, which all students needed to write and pass. I figured the worst was over, but I was very wrong. I had several night courses to re-take along with the full-time summer prep program. I failed the mock exam in July and was forced to abandon the summer and return, while my classmates went on to write the exam and pass, becoming Chartered Accountants. This failure close to the final exam was a big embarrassment, but I was forced to accept it.

I remained in purgatory until the summer of 2002, when I had to re-take the summer preparatory program alongside my girlfriend, who is now my wife. Meanwhile, I had to endure questions all year on whether I was capable of successfully graduating and becoming a Chartered Accountant. It was downright difficult to keep my mind and body up to the task. I worked hard throughout the summer of 2002, re-took the mock exam in July and passed. (Great job, Anthony, now proceed to go and collect $200!) I figured the worst was over, but again I was wrong.

I spent the next two months on self-study in preparation for the exam in September 2002—a brutal four hours per day for three wonderful days. One student collapsed just minutes before the first session began. I was so nervous that I nearly vomited every day. Luckily, I was able to keep myself composed throughout the ordeal, difficult as it was to sit down in an exam room for four hours at a stretch. I took comfort in the fact that my mother packed me a lunch each exam day (no snickering, please). Then there was the suspense of waiting till December for the results. This was the final step to becoming a Chartered Accountant—my S.M.I.L.E. was near! I figured the worst was over, but I was wrong, yet again.

When the results of the 2002 exam were announced, there was good news for my wife (she passed!) but bad news for me (I failed). Everyone around me was sad. I was distraught at their sadness, but more disappointed and embarrassed than upset at the turn of events. I remained calm since I had made an instantaneous decision to do it all over again, but that decision took a further toll on my mind and body. I drew on all the mental, physical, and emotional strength I had to succeed in my personal goal.

I took the exam again in September 2003, after several more months of self-study and leaving work for several months at my own expense. The exam was no easier this time. The methodology had changed, so my 2002 experience didn't count for much as we were being evaluated in a different manner this time. I was tested yet again, both physically and mentally. My mother said I looked like I had seen a ghost at the end of the first day (I actually had a prolonged panic attack all morning but remained at my desk and kept writing, completing the Day 1 examination paper). Panic attacks were nothing new for me, since I developed this nasty habit as a response to my anxieties about university in my second undergraduate year at McGill and they continued until I graduated. The remaining days were no easier, but I survived my dance with the 2003 exam. The results announced in December 2003 confirmed what I knew in my heart would happen: SUCCESS—I was a Chartered Accountant! I had found my S.M.I.L.E.

Conclusion: Your Body

Only with hindsight can I fully appreciate the victory, given all the mental and physical effort it required. Prepare yourself for the amount of effort your journey will demand. Always prepare for the worst and be conservative. It's better to be over-prepared than not prepared enough. Whether your journey takes one month, or seven years (as in my case), your fortitude and commitment, and your conquest of the final prize are what really matter.

"A timid person is frightened before a danger, a coward during the time, and a courageous person afterward."

– Jean Paul Richter

TEMPORARY OBSTACLE: FEAR

Preview:

- **Fear is the most significant, pervasive, and dangerous temporary obstacle you must face.**
- **To successfully find your S.M.I.L.E., you must challenge fear and emerge victorious.**

Introduction

In a memorable introduction to an episode of Seinfeld, Jerry, on stage with his usual opening monologue, tells the audience about a recent survey on people's fears. The number-one fear was public speaking, with death in second place. I love Jerry's voice as he re-emphasizes the startling results of the survey: "Death was number two!" ...and then the punch line: according to the respondents in the survey, "you are better off in the casket than giving the eulogy!"

Fear is innate. It's a powerful emotion that we're programmed with, and it influences everything from our behaviour to our investment decisions to our relationships. Sometimes, fear is perfectly understandable. If you burned your hand touching a boiling pot when you were a child, it's understandable that as an adult, you may fear boiling pots. You don't want to cause your body pain, so you'll tend to avoid boiling pots until the fear subsides. As you grow up, you learn that the way to eliminate the fear is to handle boiling pots properly by taking the necessary precautions. The fear may remain, but experience will make you less fearful so that you can handle boiling pots of water.

Fear is not so reasonable when what you fear is hypothetical scenarios in the future. If you've never burned your hand on a boiling pot of water, yet you fear the possibility of burning your hand, then your fear is really a phobia or anxiety. Fear based on a past traumatic or painful experience is understandable, but beware of phobias or anxieties, which can form barriers to experiencing life fully.

Fear is a complex topic. Let's look at the huge role it can play in your quest to unleash your full potential and find your personal success.

I firmly believe that fear is a temporary obstacle. You can tell me that you dream about your S.M.I.L.E. and that you really, really want it and I'll believe that you're sincere. You can even tell me that you feel properly prepared, both mentally and physically, for your journey to success, and I will also believe you. But if you were to tell me your fears justify not striving for your success, not fulfilling your destiny, and not finding your S.M.I.L.E., then I would find it ABSOLUTELY IMPOSSIBLE to believe you. There is no fear that can possibly justify your not reaching your maximum potential. That's why fear makes the perfect "temporary" obstacle; the nature and pervasiveness of the obstacle depend entirely on you. You alone can decide whether your fears pose no threat, set you back a little, or permanently derail your S.M.I.L.E. train.

It's all right to be scared as long as your fear doesn't prevent you from accomplishing what you set out to do. All human beings are capable of human error, because we're imperfect by nature. Don't feel sorry for yourself if you do fear something. To fear is human; to worry about things that could possibly happen or fear possible consequences or repercussions is understandable, and human. But don't disappoint yourself, your family, and your friends by letting your fears prevent you from accomplishing what you want to do. If Christopher Columbus had listened to his fears, he would never have discovered North America. If Gandhi had listened to his fears, he would never have led a spiritual revolution and pioneered the non-violent, civil disobedience that led to Indian independence. If Bill Gates had listened to his fears, we would never have been blessed with Windows (no snickering, please).

There are three main fears that I believe are the most common enemies standing in the way of achieving your maximum potential: fear of failure, fear of change, and fear of risk.

Fear is an extremely important topic, which is why I treat it so seriously and devote as much airtime as I do to it. As Napoleon Hill puts it in Think and

Grow Rich, "Fear(s) is nothing more than a state(s) of mind. One's state of mind is subject to control and direction." Once you believe that fear is just a state of mind, you'll see that it's not a huge crater but a minor speed bump as you drive to success.

Fear of Failure: Your Enemy

Have you ever been afraid of failing? Have you ever feared leaving yourself open and vulnerable? I believe we've all experienced the fear of failure at some point in our lives. In fact, fear of failure is so common that some of us face it on a daily, weekly, or monthly basis. At the physiological level, your heart beats faster, your breathing quickens, your adrenaline rises, and your muscles tense. Basically, your nervous system is uncomfortable and feels the need to boost your body's defences because your "spider-sense" is tingling. It's perfectly normal to react this way, but some people misinterpret their body's actions. For some, fear is an automatic signal that they're nearing a dangerous/uncomfortable situation and that it's best to shift into reverse and backtrack away from the situation. When you're confronted with fear, your reaction at that moment is what determines whether you fail or succeed in your mission. And this is where fear of failure rears its ugly head.

From early childhood through adolescence and on to adulthood, everyone has either feared or experienced failure. Failure can take various forms:

> *"I burned my hand on the boiling pot of water."*
>
> *"I raised my hand in class and answered the teacher's question, but I got the answer wrong."*
>
> *"I was completely committed to my boyfriend/girlfriend, but we still broke up."*
>
> *"I invested in that company but lost money."*
>
> *"I tried hard to get the promotion but I wasn't successful."*
>
> *"Our first year in business we were very successful, but in our second year, business declined dramatically."*

Each of these common scenarios depicts a failure. You may have even found yourself repeating one or several of these statements in your life. Keep reminding yourself that to err is human. It's perfectly all right to make a mistake and fail when confronted with a situation. Fear of failure is acceptable. What's not acceptable is making the same mistake a second time. Strive to learn from your failure as quickly as possible. Failure stinks, of course. It's a certifiable downer, but it happens. And when it does happen, you must have the proper attitude to accept it—as cold and calculated as a surgeon in the operating room, able to separate emotion from logical reasoning. Don't kid yourself, this is much more difficult than it appears. You can train yourself to react in a logical, focused, and objective manner when faced with fear and conquer it. All it takes is a little practice. See the Strategies section for tips on confronting your fears. I believe that armed with these tools, you can bring fear to its knees. You can program yourself to respond to the challenge of fear. The objective is to make the right choice, regardless of any fear you may encounter.

Fear of failure is particularly nasty because it robs you of pleasure. Fear of failure frequently stops you from performing an action due to the possible consequences. The child who burns her hand on a boiling pot may avoid cooking for fear of getting burned (failure). The student may stop raising his hand in class for fear of embarrassing himself again by giving the wrong answer in front of classmates (failure). The teenager may not date for a long time to avoid further heartbreak (failure). The worker may stop performing, believing that promotion is unattainable (failure). Business partners may dissolve the company because their second year was horrible (failure).

Each of the original scenarios presented a failure. Each of these new scenarios shows the possible, unfortunate consequences of failing once. The unfortunate consequence is when fear of failure shows its dangerous side and robs you of pleasure. In each of the second set of scenarios, the person has failed and is close to calling it quits, fearing the experience of further displeasure.

This is normal because as humans, we're constantly seeking pleasure. Whether it's eating our favourite foods or doing our favourite activities, we want to have fun and we hate things that bring pain. So, at the physiological level, it's normal for the mind and body to fear going out on a date after your heart's been broken. Yet this is precisely when you must be your strongest. This is when you must be objective and collected, like the surgeon. You must know where you are, what it is you want, and how to get it.

A colleague of mine who was in the Canadian Armed Forces described a typical day in the army. Nothing is left to chance. Soldiers go through rigorous training so they know instinctively what to expect and how to react when faced with danger. My colleague explained the various procedures used to transport important personnel through dangerous enemy terrain. I was amazed. I learned that soldiers are prepared for anything; therefore, despite their fears they instinctively know what course of action to take when faced with a decision. Commercial airline pilots undergo training with the same concept in mind. Pilots spend thousands of hours in flight simulators to recreate the conditions they can expect at the helm of a real aircraft. Nothing is left to chance. Before becoming a soldier or a pilot, the candidate may have feared some aspect of the new profession, but with proper training, they were able to overcome their fear and perform as they should: at 100%.

Prepare for your quest for your S.M.I.L.E. as if you were a soldier or a pilot. Your objective is clear: to stay cool, calm and collected to minimize the effect of fear.

Earlier in the book, I emphasized the importance of the Guarantee, Completion Certificate, Objectives, and Steps—tools that are of the utmost importance for your journey. The Guarantee is a promise to yourself, based on your dreams and desire. The Objective is the final prize: your S.M.I.L.E. Both play important roles in your preparations as they indicate your destination. Like a soldier, pilot, or surgeon, knowing your destination in advance helps focus your mind and body to the task at hand. While you prepare to find your S.M.I.L.E., outline the steps you believe are necessary to reach your goal. Everything must be laid out in advance (as we did in Phase I: Planning) so that once you arrive at Phase II: Executing, you know exactly what you have to do.

Great, Anthony, but how does this tie in with our fear of failure? I'm happy you asked that question. Fear of failure occurs when you fear the possible negative outcome of your actions for fear of being branded a "loser." Being classified a failure is just too difficult for some people. They feel there's a stigma associated with failure and they'll suffer a severe blow to their reputation. I do sympathize with this thought pattern, but it's flawed. Yet I'm not surprised that so many people have this thought pattern programmed into their minds.

Robert Kiyosaki (author of *Rich Dad Poor Dad*) points out that we're trained from elementary school to university to avoid mistakes at all costs. Mistakes are frowned upon and are "bad." Like Kiyosaki, I believe that schools train us to be mindless machines, seeking to avoid error. I've learned my best lessons from failure and gained countless experiences from my mistakes. I've made so many mistakes in my life that it feels normal to fail and learn something immediately afterward. I wish this were not the case, since failure can sometimes be a tough pill to swallow, but I have no regrets. Kiyosaki says that schools are adept at producing employees but not entrepreneurs. Entrepreneurs don't let fear of failure keep them on the sidelines. Entrepreneurs are visionaries who shun the notion of failure, embrace risk, and set out on their path despite what the so-called "experts" say. Kiyosaki quotes the famous football player Fran Tarkenton: "Winners are not afraid of losing."

Fear of Change: Your Enemy

Fear of change is closely linked to fear of risk, and both types of fear are very common in today's society. Change can be very difficult to deal with, since staying with the status quo is usually much more comfortable.

> "The difficulty lies not so much in developing new ideas as in escaping from the old ones."
> – *John Maynard Keynes*

It takes energy to change. A body at rest remains at rest unless you apply energy to force it to move. Similarly, if a body is in motion, then it remains in motion until you apply energy to stop it. Based on this logic, it's understandable that humans aren't fond of change, which requires effort. Faced with a choice between expending energy and changing or staying put and not changing, which choice requires less effort? Not changing, of course.

I believe most people who don't take steps to achieve their S.M.I.L.E. are simply too afraid of change. Let's say you're working in a job you dislike. It's easier to continue working in the job you dislike than to seek out a different one. After all, there are all your friends at work, and the salary and benefits aren't too bad, and it's not like you'd be much happier elsewhere.

The previous sentence shows how your brain rationalizes your decisions, so that you convince yourself that though you're unhappy with your current work situation, the devil you know is better than the devil you don't know.

In social psychology, this behaviour comes under the category of cognitive dissonance theory. To summarize the theory, where there is tension/disaccord between two beliefs, your mind will seek to reduce the tension. Therefore, given that a new job would make you happier, and you're not happy with your current job, the obvious action/belief would be to leave your current job and find a new one. However, what happens when you don't act upon your belief? Here is where we see the tension/disaccord. Your current situation says: "I am still in the same job." The tension stems from the fact that you know you need to change jobs, but you lack the willpower to search for a new one. Therefore, you are in disaccord. You should be looking elsewhere, but you aren't. Ironically, your mind may attempt to rationalize your contradictory behaviour—not being satisfied with your current job, yet not seeking a change.

Cognitive theory holds that the intensity of one of the beliefs will be diluted. You'll obviously want to hold the beliefs that require less effort to achieve. You will likely convince yourself that your current job isn't "too bad" by rationalizing your displeasures, explaining away your dissatisfaction with the current position, since it's much easier to stay in the same rut than to seek out new work. Not changing lets you carry on with the current routine, whereas finding a new job would require contacting new people, marketing yourself, and enduring several interviews before settling into a new position—all barriers.

Attacking the beliefs that "a new job will make me happier" and that you are "not happy with your current job" is much easier than looking for a new job. That's a tragedy because you become much more comfortable with accepting the status quo as opposed to challenging yourself to get what you want. Whether your fear of change is psychological or physiological, seek out change instead of settling for your current lot. It may be easy to go along with the status quo, but is that what you really want?

Weight loss is another example of putting up with your current condition rather than seeking a change. Changing your physical appearance because you're overweight takes effort and sacrifice. Some people view the effort required as an insurmountable goal and put up with the status quo instead. They won't change because it requires too much effort, despite their unhappiness with their current physique. And that's a tragedy, because the fear of change overpowers the desire for change. Your dreams and your desire are your companions on the journey to success, your allies when you face your most significant temporary obstacle (fear), and your helpers in focusing your mind and body in one constant direction (towards success). Use the website tools to reinforce the intensity of your dreams and desire. To help with your mental/physical preparation in Phase II—Execution, use the website tools that involve clearly stating your objectives and the steps it will take to achieve those objectives. Focus your mind and body and address your fears with the techniques outlined in the Strategies section.

Change isn't easy. It takes energy and effort to make change happen. Change can yield good things, but it can also lead to a more difficult situation. Change carries an element of risk. But aren't you willing to take a chance on changing yourself, changing your habits or your lifestyle for the better? Isn't that worth fighting for? Can you put a price tag on your happiness? I can't. I value personal freedom and happiness for myself, my family and my friends more than anything in the world. Look at your efforts to effect change as an investment. In life, you will face unfavourable circumstances that you must put up with. "Insanity is doing the SAME thing and expecting a different result," writes the famous author Anonymous. If something fails miserably the first time, you can either adapt or die. You don't have to change everything, but you may have to make some modifications. What should NOT change are your desire, persistence, and dedication to getting it right.

As Robert Kiyosaki notes in his Rich Dad Poor Dad series, happiness can be yours, but you must be willing to "pay the price." While some say he is too general and fails to give specific steps that lead to being "free," I believe the series goes into sufficient detail on the benefits of financial freedom. Follow the steps I outline here, in sequence, and you'll become your very own success story! Find inspiration wherever you can, from this book, Kiyosaki, or Robbins' tapes, to pave the way to your "road-to-riches" S.M.I.L.E. journey. Your S.M.I.L.E. will be yours forever, so you must be convinced that your journey is worth the effort. Yes, it will take effort to change. Yes, change is always uncertain, but apart from death and taxes, what else is certain in life?

Fear of Risk (Inherent to the Fear of Change)

I spent several years as a risk management consultant for a Big 4 Accounting firm and various Canadian public companies. My area of expertise was financial information risk, but the lessons learned in this discipline can easily be applied to the general concept of risk. You can't eliminate risk, only minimize it. It's optimistic and incorrect to describe anything as being "risk-free"—a term frequently used in advertisements and commercials. There's always that element of the "unknown" in life.

If a commercial proudly proclaims a risk-free trial period for the product, they're only telling half the truth. The manufacturer may offer a 30-day trial period, during which dissatisfied customers can get their money back with no questions asked. But you're still taking a risk. What if the company goes bankrupt during the 30-day trial period? How do you get your money back? What if the company moves to a foreign country without leaving a forwarding address? How likely are you to get your refund? Risk is inherent in everything, no matter what you do. Get comfortable with that fact, like Neo in The Matrix: "Welcome to the real world (reality)."

Risk is everywhere. You can't eliminate risk, but you can take steps to prevent and reduce it. Driving your car is risky, but by observing the speed limit and buckling your seat belt, you reduce the risk of accidents and serious injuries. Cycling and rollerblading are risky, so you wear safety equipment.

> "There are risks and costs to a program of action. But they are far less than the long-range risks and costs of comfortable inaction."
>
> *– John F. Kennedy*

How does risk affect the quest for your S.M.I.L.E.? I simply hope you understand that your fear of change is deceptive. It's holding you back from succeeding. Fear of change prevents you from reaching your full potential. So don't believe yourself if your fear of change tries to discourage you from pursuing your journey, attempting to trick your mind and saying it's too "risky" to change yourself for the better, try to improve yourself, and find your S.M.I.L.E. That's simply not true.

"If you don't risk anything you risk even more."

– Erica Jong

"The policy of being too cautious is the greatest risk of all."

– Jawaharlal Nehru

Imagine that you're overweight. Now imagine that your dream is to lose weight and feel great. You know you'll have to pay a "price"—let's say waking up early and going to the gym every day. We've identified your objective (weight loss), we know what steps are required (daily workouts), and we know you desire this S.M.I.L.E. for yourself.

Now let's look at your fears. You may fear failure—it would be no fun to fail this quest. You may fear change: "What if I don't look better?" or "What if my health/figure doesn't improve?" and "What if I do all this for nothing?" The risks could be the cost of a gym membership (several hundred dollars), your time (priceless), and the risk to your confidence and self-esteem if you fail.

But what about the risks associated with not changing? Believe it or not, opting for the status quo can be much riskier. Being overweight puts a strain on your heart, increases your changes of developing illnesses, and takes a toll on your body. Isn't that risky? As we've seen, you can't avoid risk. Taking a chance and wanting to change carries just as much risk as settling for the status quo—accepting the fact that you're overweight and placing your health at risk. Do you see the irony? Both choices involve risk. Yet which choice carries a greater risk? I'm sure you'll realize that not pursuing your dream of getting into shape carries a greater risk for your body and your self-esteem than the risk of trying and failing. Which risk are you more comfortable with?

MORE ON RISK

Spencer Johnson: Who Moved My Cheese?

Johnson uses the analogy of mice caught in a maze to illustrate the effects fear of change has on the human psyche. Mice in one section of a maze have a supply of cheese, but their food stocks are rapidly dwindling. Here's where the plot thickens. Some mice decide that to survive, they must venture out to find a new supply of cheese or risk eating all the remaining cheese and eventually starving. Another group of mice dismiss the idea as too "risky" and decide it's a better idea to manage the dwindling food supply rather than brave the unknown. Eventually, one group sets off into the maze in search of cheese while the other group stays put, sticking with the "devil they know" (the rapidly depleting cheese supply) as opposed to the "devil they don't know."

This analogy illustrates the difference between risk-averse people and risk-takers. Risk-averse people would rather remain in their current situation regardless of the consequences. The group of mice who were unwilling to leave and look for more cheese were content to stay on their current path even though it would endanger their lives. The other group of mice felt it would be better to risk venturing out in the maze in search of cheese than to accept their current fate and be doomed. Granted, it took courage to make this decision but was it really as "risky" as the mice who stayed behind believed?

Sometimes opting for what seems like a sure thing (the current supply of cheese) versus the unknown (possible alternative sources of cheese) seems like a safer choice, but is actually the riskier course. Presumably, the risk-taking mice were eventually rewarded with an alternative supply of cheese and lived happily ever after. The story may be simplistic, but it shows that sometimes taking what looks like a risk can be the best option. Fear of change can be a hurdle you'll have to overcome to find your S.M.I.L.E. and succeed.

The Immigrant Story

How would you react if you realized that you needed to relocate to a different country with your spouse and your children? You'd have to sell all your possessions, keeping only what you could carry (did I mention that you're taking a boat?). The trip is long, and the climate in your new country is much colder than in your native country. You don't speak either of the two official languages in your new country, so you'll have to struggle with career opportunities (don't expect any executive positions) and your children may find school hard at first. Your whole family will have to adapt. And you can't go back, because you've sold everything and there's very little opportunity for advancement in your home country. The big plus is that you'll be with your large extended family (that is a plus, right?) and there are opportunities for work—arduous physical labour.

Does this sound like an enormous challenge? It does to me, but these are just a few of the challenges immigrants face. I've just described the difficult decision my father's parents, like thousands of others, faced in the 1950s when they decided to leave southern Italy for Canada. Facing political uncertainties and a lack of opportunities in Italy, my grandparents believed emigration was their only alternative. They had heard wonderful stories of Canada, the land of opportunity. Was it better to stay with the "devil they knew" (lack of opportunity in Italy) or tackle the "devil they didn't know" (a new life in Canada)?

Obviously, fear of failure, fear of change, and fear of risk figured in my grandparents' decision. If their gamble failed, they could be condemned to live in even greater poverty. They faced a long list of temporary obstacles (see above). Selling nearly all your belongings and taking your family across the Atlantic Ocean to a place where you have no guarantee of work or investment opportunities is clearly a significant risk. But wasn't it even riskier to stay behind and accept certain poverty and lack of progress? Although emigration appeared to be extremely risky, it would also have been very risky to stay in poor conditions, with no opportunity for advancement. And so leaving Italy for North America was the only viable alternative.

My father often told me how difficult it was for him growing up. He and his brother were teased at school for being different, and employment meant manual labour and other low-paying jobs. Yet despite of the challenges, I believe my father's family turned out all right: they purchased property, accumulated modest savings, and raised a family. My mother's family went through a similar immigrant experience, and they were also able to adapt and make a decent living for future generations. My grandparents and parents worked very hard to provide for the current generation, and for that we are very grateful.

But let's not forget our discussion on fear. For both families, the decision to leave southern Italy must have seemed like an emotional roller coaster. It meant confronting all the fears we've been discussing: fear of failure, change, and risk. It took courage to leave Italy, and my grandparents had to face their fear of failure. The consequences of failure would also have affected their sons, my father and his brother, but they triumphed over their fears and made the move. Leaving their home in southern Italy for an unfamiliar country thousands of kilometres away meant having to deal with change and new surroundings—an intimidating prospect and a huge obstacle to face. They conquered their fear of change and pursued their dreams and desire for a better life. Leaving was the biggest risk they would ever take in their lives, but it actually proved to be beneficial for them and for future generations. However big or small your temporary obstacles appear to be, never forget the immigrant story. Remember that you or someone you know has faced every one of the fears you face in choosing your path in life. No decision is ever easy. But if you have dreams, desire and a destiny to S.M.I.L.E., nothing can deter you from your ultimate goal.

Conclusion: Fear

Fear is the most significant temporary obstacle. Incredibly, Bill Clinton, former president of the United States, still feels slightly nervous before delivering a big speech. The lesson here is that it's acceptable to be fearful or nervous—it shows you're human. It also shows that you care about what you're doing. Clinton delivers important speeches despite his nerves, which shows that fear is normal. But don't let it dictate your agenda.

Fear of failure, change, and risk are barbarians you're sure to encounter on your journey. They'll appear to be bigger, stronger and more powerful than you are, but remember everything we've discussed in this chapter, and arm yourself with the strategies in the next section. Along with your dreams and desires and your mind and body, they will help you triumph over your fears. Fears can be conquered. Once you conquer a fear, it won't return—it won't stand a chance. Look your fears in the face courageously. Once you conquer your fears, you'll realize that they were never that powerful to begin with!

MIND STRATEGY: CONFIDENCE

Preview

- **Confidence is your friend.**
- **Confidence is an ally for your mind.**
- **Call on your confidence, develop it, and use it properly to unlock your full potential.**

Introduction

In a 2006 broadcast, radio personality Colin Cowherd (ESPN Radio's "The Herd with Colin Cowherd") summarized confidence in the most succinct, interesting, and effective manner I've ever heard. He said that confidence is one of those intangibles that are difficult to explain, even more difficult to quantify, and extremely difficult to control. However, no athlete can deny its existence. You can see the difference that confidence makes in (athletic) performance when you see one team playing with confidence and the other lacking confidence. The difference can be astounding.

Confidence is intangible. I believe it has to do with your instincts. You know when you have it, and you definitely know when you don't. Ask any athlete how difficult it is to face an opponent that's playing with a high level of confidence. It doesn't matter if one team is ranked highly and the other team is ranked low, since a weaker team playing with confidence can be just as difficult an adversary as a highly ranked team.

Confidence: Why Do I Need It?

Confidence is not the be-all-end-all factor that determines the ultimate success of your performance, but you can't deny its importance. At some point in your journey to your personal success, you will need confidence—an important ally for your mind on your mission to find your S.M.I.L.E. When someone is confident, the confidence is like a perfume that permeates every pore of that person's body. Have you ever seen the way a confident person acts? They wear a huge smile, and walk with square shoulders. They move like a puma, with smooth, gliding steps, fully aware of their surroundings and environment. They have a rhythm all to themselves, and can do no wrong.

What's even more interesting is how people react when they meet a person who exudes confidence. It's extremely difficult to deny the wishes of a highly confident individual. A confident person is fully aware of their "hot streak." Sales reps will tell you that when they're hot, they're unstoppable. Confidence helps you translate your efforts into results. I don't believe there's a direct correlation between confidence and success, but there is a correlation and it is not to be ignored. Be aware of confidence, and the feelings it can give you. Being in the confidence zone is an amazing feeling. It's your objective to find that zone and stay there as long as you can. Feeling confident is an indicator of opportune times—it means you're "on fire," so be sure you "strike while the iron is hot."

Anthony's True Confession No. 5: ***I stink at gambling. I'm invited to tournaments to make "donations" to the other players at the table.***

Professional gamblers swear by confidence. They can wait for hours at a poker table, knowing the best time to strike. The difference between professional gamblers and amateurs like me can be seen in the decisions they make at these opportune moments. Amateurs constantly mis-time their bets, taking on more risk than they need to. Professional gamblers may wait all night for that moment when they feel the stars are aligned—they feel confident, the odds are in their favour, and they see an opportunity—but when that moment does arrive, they don't hesitate to place heavy bets, knowing that now's the moment to maximize their winnings.

In the course of your journey, I'm certain you'll find yourself more confident at some times than others. Cherish those moments, the times when you'll make significant progress towards finding your S.M.I.L.E. These moments of maximum confidence are precisely when you must attack. Take chances during these periods of high confidence because your mind is telling you that your engine is revved up. It's a sign that all systems are go, so obey the signals and make your move now.

Confidence is your ally—one of those ingredients you need just the right amount of to find the perfect recipe. People won't notice whether you have any confidence unless you have enough of it, but everyone will notice if you possess too much confidence. You don't want to be categorized as one of those over-confident people who talk too much and brag about their talents.

What's the right amount of confidence? Strive for humility—an undervalued quality in today's world. I value humility in myself and those around me. Humble people realize their place in life. When you're around an over-confident braggart, inevitably the conversation revolves around them and their exploits. You'll soon grow tired of talking to over-confident people, since they're self-centered and selfish. Humble people take both negative and positive feedback in stride, accept things for what they are, and have the silent confidence to know what they want and how hard they have to work to get it.

This is how you should strive to market yourself in the confidence spectrum—right in the middle. Being over-confident is just as harmful as not being confident enough. I believe your spouse, family, and friends will come to admire, appreciate, and value you for all your qualities if you have enough confidence to stay in that mid range of self-confidence.

Anthony, how do I develop my confidence?

I hope I've convinced you that confidence is your friend and that it's indispensable in your journey to success. Now let's look at how to boost and maintain your confidence, and what to do when your confidence seems to be slipping away.

I believe you'll find yourself in the "I need to get confident because…." zone quite often—and that's absolutely normal. You'll find yourself in that zone once you embark on your voyage to finding your S.M.I.L.E. or when you're faced with a temporary obstacle. Here's the mind-set: you need to boost your confidence because you realize there are obstacles ahead. You realize that you need to develop more confidence to successfully complete this phase of your journey and reach the next objective. Don't despair; this is an extremely common state of mind. You'll need energy (remember our physics lesson?) to get moving in the desired direction. I believe that there are two extremely simple ways to boost your confidence: practice and small victories.

Practice means repeating the steps it takes to reach your goal over and over until they seem automatic, so you can nearly do them in your sleep. In risk management, we call this a walk-through. I'll use the terms interchangeably as they mean the same thing.

Success requires practice. As athletes like to say, "If you fail to prepare, prepare to fail." Olympic athletes will tell you that they devote years of their life to preparing for a single event, though it may take only minutes to complete. So if you ever feel compelled to complain about the amount of practice/preparation required to find your S.M.I.L.E., remember all the people out there who work harder and longer than you to achieve their dreams and desires. Use that thought to motivate you during your practices, keep your spirits up, and stay motivated.

You'll also need confidence to keep your mind tuned to your S.M.I.L.E. radio station. You must remain confident to make sure your mind stays focused on the objectives you've set for yourself using the website tools. You must remain 100% focused because there's a temporary obstacle (fear) lurking around the corner and it's your mind's greatest enemy. It will stop at nothing to defeat you in times of weakness and despair. Remaining confident will help you weather the storm of fear—fear of failure or fear of change. Confidence will tell your fears to go away—and they will. Then you'll be free to continue on your journey to your S.M.I.L.E.

Now, what is it about practice that boosts your confidence? I like the repetition associated with practice. Do you find repetition boring? Do you feel that if you repeat something often enough you can do it backwards, upside down, and in Latin? With enough practice, don't you find that tasks become repetitive and devoid of challenge? Good! Embrace that feeling—it's the key to building your confidence.

Anthony's Real-Life Example: Confidence in Public Speaking

Setback: ***natural nervousness and fear of failure***

Lesson learned: ***practice produces confidence.***

I've always enjoyed public speaking. I've always loved the challenge of preparing a speech, practicing it over and over, and delivering it in front of an audience with the goal of making it both interesting and amusing. I wish every public speaker would take this as seriously as I do.

When I'm getting ready for a public-speaking engagement, I prepare myself thoroughly, whether my audience is school children or baby boomers. I practice and practice to develop a certain level of confidence. I don't want to come across as over-confident, arrogant, or cocky, because that would turn off my audience. On the other hand, I don't want to find myself under-prepared, which would make me more anxious and detract from my performance. I strongly recommend over-preparation so that you approach the task at hand feeling appropriately confident, yet humble at the same time, as you've invested so much of your own time in preparing for the engagement. Mentally, you're giving the speaking engagement the respect it deserves, which puts you in the proper mind-set to be an effective public speaker. Practice makes perfect.

I compose several drafts of my speech well in advance, then polish my final draft. I read the speech over and over until I know it would make my brain hurt to read it one more time. Finally, I proceed to the memorization phase. I stand up (honestly) and repeat the second step, reading/saying the speech over and over until this too becomes too boring to endure.

Eventually, after the repeated walk-throughs of reading and rehearsing my speech, I try to recite the words from memory. I don't worry about perfect repetition at this point, but I do focus on saying as much as I can without looking down at my notes. Occasionally I'll notice that I've deviated from the script, but I don't worry too much since my main objective is to continue practicing my speech. The repetition serves to ingrain the words in my mind so that I can recite most of my speech without using my notes.

I do refer to my notes during my oral presentation, just to make sure I've said everything I wanted to say in the right sequence and raised all the points I intended to raise. Even with all the practice and my notes as a visual aid, I may still make the odd mistake in front of the audience. Yes, this is fear of failure. However, since I've spent so much time practicing, the likelihood (risk) of errors happening is significantly reduced. This frees my mind to focus on more interesting challenges, such as embellishing my speech with improved vocabulary, conveying the appropriate facial expressions during the presentation, and executing flawlessly.

Sometimes laughter, heckling, or other unforeseen circumstances have interrupted me during a presentation. This is normal. Factor this into your preparation. It's fine to practice under ideal circumstances, but much more effective to practice under less-than-ideal circumstances, since the reality usually lies somewhere in between. It's a good idea to practice while you're distracted by television or radio. This will serve you well, preparing you for possible distractions during the real performance while still letting you test yourself in a practice environment.

Confidence sets your brain free to be creative and focus on the task at hand, since it doesn't have to combat fear. This is when you are most effective. This is how to find your S.M.I.L.E. Make it easy on yourself by investing the time it takes to develop a solid routine of practice. Let your brain practice "succeeding" by performing the task over and over. This forces you to deliver in a comfortable setting, and develops your confidence.

Small Victories

Another way to practice success is through small victories or easy tasks. Do you, like me, prepare a to-do list and enjoy the feeling of crossing off each task? It's a good feeling to know that you've accomplished something, whether the task is large or small. The strategy of small victories involves setting up small tasks to complete that are either directly or indirectly related to achieving your S.M.I.L.E.

Here's an example: Say that your major overall goal is to deliver a successful speech to an audience of 100 people. The strategy of small victories would involve completing several speaking engagements to small groups, gradually working your way up to 100 people. You could start off speaking to a group of two people, then four, 10, 40, 75, and finally 100 people. Every experience in front of a live audience will enhance your confidence because you'll approach each speaking engagement in the same manner. You have to practice your speech over and over, regardless of the size of the audience. The advantage of practicing in front of small audiences and gradually increasing the size of the audience is that it lets you perfect your performance without having to deliver immediately in front of 100 people. I'm certain you'll be much more comfortable speaking before an audience of two people first instead of proceeding directly to the group of 100. Gradually increasing the difficulty of a set task lets you test yourself slowly and lets your mind familiarize itself with the feeling of speaking in front of a live audience of whatever size.

The key concept in accomplishing small victories/easy tasks in succession is building confidence. Is this a simple way of gradually increasing your confidence? Absolutely. Is it effective? Without a doubt. Why does a strategy have to be complicated? Never underestimate how effective it can be to successfully complete a series of simple tasks and boost your confidence. There's nothing wrong with using these simple tasks to perfect your approach and improve your delivery.

MORE ON CONFIDENCE AND EXPERIENCE

Robert Kiyosaki: Rich Dad Poor Dad

Kiyosaki suggests gaining experience in a similar way. He uses the example of investing in real estate. Kiyosaki says that people want to move too far too fast when investing. He quotes that famous proverb, "A journey of a thousand steps begins with a single step." One step isn't much, but it represents the initial motion towards your destination. Kiyosaki believes a journey of a thousand steps can start with a baby step—you can still accomplish great feats simply by making a tiny initial effort in the right direction.

Kiyosaki feels that amateur investors want to do too much too soon and jump on that big "perfect" deal. The problem with that way of thinking is that without practice, amateur investors can't handle the deal. It would be too much for them to absorb (large investment required, complex transaction, or some other variable) all at once. He advocates starting early, practicing, developing your skills, and learning as much as you can. That way, you'll gain more experience than the investor waiting on the sidelines who isn't learning anything. Experience is golden. I couldn't have said it better myself.

Know Yourself and Act Accordingly

Another strategy, which I call playing to your own personal preference, involves knowing yourself, being aware of your personal momentum, and shuffling the timing so that it plays to your strengths. I'm a certified morning person. I can think clearly, react quickly, concentrate, and deal with distraction better in the morning than in the afternoon or evening. I did all my studying in the morning because I noticed over the years that my concentration level plummets dramatically as the day progresses. The sharpest decline is after lunch. Knowing this about myself, I scheduled all my homework assignments and studying in the morning, playing to my strengths. Obviously, I usually studied alone because most of my classmates were night owls. I knew it was vital for me to complete my reading assignments and other class work before lunch or risk either falling asleep over my books or having to finish the work the next day.

In your quest for your S.M.I.L.E., build your confidence by playing to your strengths. If you work better late at night, do your work then. Why make life more difficult for yourself by doing important things at inopportune times? When you have the choice, let your personal preferences dictate the schedule for your efforts. You'll be doing yourself a favour. Your mind and body will thank you for it.

Maintaining Your Confidence

It's fun to find yourself performing well, with plenty of confidence. Your objective is to perform consistently at an optimal level and succeed at what you set out to do. When that's happening, you may well wonder how long can this last. Aim to operate at a maximum level of confidence and effectiveness. Athletes say it's easier to become number one than to stay in the top spot. With practice and hard work, a boxer can win the title fight and be crowned champion. However, once you're the champ, you're the prime target of challengers everywhere who want their title shot. There are obvious challenges involved in being at the top of your game, but remember that's the best zone—the place you want to find yourself. The challenge lies not in getting yourself ready for the challenges but maintaining your performance level, since you're already operating the way you should.

What's the secret of staying confident? Your approach to maintaining your confidence mirrors the approach you take to building your confidence: practice and small victories. Focus your energy on maintaining your current momentum. Tiger Woods works just as hard today as he did when attempting to qualify for the PGA Tour. Michael Jordan worked just as hard when his Chicago Bulls were winning championships as when they were trying to win their first championship. It may sound simplistic, but don't discount the importance of maintaining your practice routine and working on improving your execution. To remain confident, you must keep on delivering quality results, so maintain the same level of intensity in your practice sessions. Set up easy tasks that become increasingly difficult to gear yourself up for game time. Remember, even though you're confident, it's vital to maintain that level and make confidence your partner on your journey to success. What better way to remain confident than to practice hard, work hard, and develop your execution with small victories?

Recovering Your Confidence (or Preventing It From Slipping Away Further)

This is the second most common confidence zone you'll find yourself in on your journey. Let's take golf for an example. Golf is a sport that requires you to execute your swing in the same manner as consistently as possible. Unfortunately, some holes may prove to be more difficult than others, depending on the hole layout, slope, or speed of the green, no matter how well you're hitting the ball.

Golf is all about risk and reward. Sometimes you're well rewarded for taking risky shots, and sometimes you're penalized for attempting low-probability shots. Obviously, professional golfers invest an inordinate amount of time in perfecting their technique and skills. Golfers realize that their play tends to improve when they're playing confidently and their game deteriorates as their confidence gets shaky. So the question remains: How do you regain your confidence when you see your momentum shift for the worse?

The first thing to do if you feel you're losing your confidence on your path towards your S.M.I.L.E. is realize that it's normal to feel that way. Don't be too hard on yourself. What's paramount is how you respond to the challenge of a falling confidence level. Let's go back to the golf analogy for a moment. Every golfer can tell you about moments when he was confident through a series of holes and then, for some unknown reason and in an instant, a momentum change—for the worse—occurred. At this point, the golfer found himself struggling to regain his confidence and recapture his

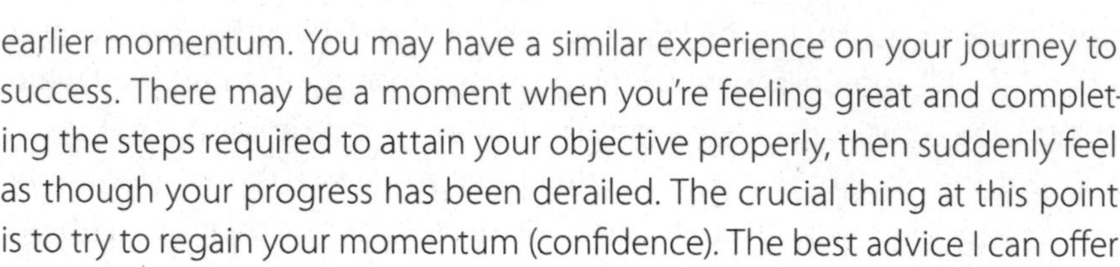

earlier momentum. You may have a similar experience on your journey to success. There may be a moment when you're feeling great and completing the steps required to attain your objective properly, then suddenly feel as though your progress has been derailed. The crucial thing at this point is to try to regain your momentum (confidence). The best advice I can offer here is to slow down and maintain your focus.

Why slow down? Because you're currently in an uphill battle. Since a turn of events has caused you to relinquish some momentum, try to recover that lost momentum to return to full strength. Your lost confidence has increased the odds against you. All is not lost, but your likelihood of success has decreased slightly and the cards are no longer in your favour as you want them to be. Professional gamblers don't bet everything they have on a hand if they feel they don't hold the advantage. Professionals wager heavily when probabilities are in their favour. Why should you be any different? If you feel there's been either a momentum change or a drop in your confidence level, why feel the need to risk everything? Amateur gamblers would tell you to disregard such internal warning signs and bet hard, as if nothing had ever happened. They would tell you to disregard your instincts and continue with the attack.

I totally disagree with that approach. If your body is telling you something is wrong, why risk everything? If your spider-sense is tingling, why ignore it? That doesn't mean you must abandon everything and run for the hills, because that's cowardly and arguably the riskiest strategy of all. But if you feel you're no longer in control of a situation, slow it down. Let your body rhythm adjust to the new circumstances. Obviously, try your best to regain your confidence as quickly as possible.

Once you feel back in control and feel that the odds are again in your favour, continue to apply your maximum efforts and fire on all cylinders. In golf, there's a saying that managing your bad holes is just as important as scoring on easy holes. I firmly believe you must take advantage of any opportunity that presents itself. Yes, sometimes, a missed opportunity will return, but not always. Why wait for a second opportunity when you can hammer out a victory the first time? Why risk waiting?

Likewise, going back to our golf analogy, there are those moments when crisis management becomes as important as seizing opportunity. In golf, every stroke counts. A two-foot putt is just as important as a 200-yard drive. In both cases, your objective is to complete a hole in the lowest number of strokes. There will be times when the road suddenly appears to be bumpier than it was before. All of a sudden, you aren't performing as well as you were previously. This is evidence of a decrease in momentum (confidence). Slow it down. There's no need to go any faster than required. You're perfectly within your rights to measure each of your subsequent actions to make sure they're consistent with achieving your objectives. Manage the bad holes. This means not inflicting any damage to yourself in the process. Don't waste any strokes. They'll come back to haunt you. Golfers hate wasted strokes because they stay on your scorecard for the entire round. Gamblers will tell you they hate losing more money than they had to because of a bad play.

It's all right to make mistakes and suffer a setback or loss, but it's not in your best interest to compound the negative turn of events by losing more. Does a sinking ship help its cause by taking on more water than it has to? Slow it down. Stop the bleeding. Don't make any more serious mistakes than need be. Slowing down gives your mind a chance to adjust, refocus, and return to its previous, more confident state. Be your own best friend. Know yourself well enough to know when it's time to get aggressive and when it's time to simplify things. When your mind is saying it feels unsure, this is no time to complicate things. Give your mind some extra time to collect itself and refocus by progressing slowly. Once you've regained your focus and your confidence, you'll be able to function at maximum efficiency again.

Confidence: Conclusion

Confidence is difficult to characterize and even more difficult to control, but never underestimate its importance. Confidence is real; luckily, it's your ally. Call upon your confidence to make your dreams a reality. You'll need confidence to combat your fears and help your mind as you move ahead on your journey. Use these strategies to make sure you're at one with your confidence, whether you have too little of it, too much, or (preferably) just the right amount.

MIND STRATEGY: VOCABULARY

Preview

- **Effective vocabulary is your friend.**
- **Effective vocabulary is an ally for your mind.**
- **Use a winner's vocabulary, complete with positive words, affirmations, and concrete solutions.**

Introduction

This section is smaller than the other chapters, but I hope you'll find some useful insights in these pages. Basically, I believe that your vocabulary helps direct your mind to the proper path through positive thinking. You can't be a pessimist and still believe you will succeed, because the odds are significantly against negativity. Negative people bring bad karma to themselves and those around them. Don't be a naysayer. The comedian George Lopez often asks the question: "Are you a Mexi-can or a Mexi-can't?" Do you believe you can or can't do things? You must be able to answer questions in the affirmative. I love the word "yes." I detest the word "no."

Words influence your mind. Negative words have a pervasive effect on your focus. Avoid negativity at all costs. A positive vocabulary provides insight into what you're feeling in your soul. Vocabulary influences your mind and makes it believe what you want it to believe. When you look at a situation and take either a positive or negative viewpoint, what you observe will obviously be different depending on the viewpoint chosen. Always try to put a positive spin on things, which makes it much easier for the mind to absorb and process. Negativity is cancer. Avoid bad karma. Being positive and using a winner's vocabulary will help your mind enjoy the beauty of your journey. A winner's vocabulary is rife with adjectives (positive descriptive words), affirmations, and solutions.

Adjectives

I adore using positive adjectives to describe things in life. Words like "fantastic," "fabulous," and "excellent" frequently appear in my vocabulary. Yes, sometimes I use them as a reflex, but in most cases I mean what I say. I like using positive adjectives because they embellish the good aspects of things. If I had a great time at golf with my buddies, I'll say I had an "amazing" time. If an espresso is very good, I'll say it's "fantastic." My mission in life is to maximize the good and minimize the bad. It's all about perception. Vocabulary lets you put a "spin" on feelings, events, and people, too. Don't hesitate to add spin—politicians do it all the time. How often do you see politicians complain in their campaign speeches? They generally focus on the positive—what they want to bring to the electorate. True, campaigns are sometimes fought in the trenches, which is unfortunate. However, normally politicians sanitize their messages to make everything sound rosy and easily digestible by the general public. Words are extremely powerful. Use positive adjectives to maximize your pleasure. Treat your mind by embellishing all the good things in life.

You can also use adjectives to minimize the effect of negative events. Downplay the importance of unfavourable circumstances to convince your mind that the displeasure really isn't that bad. Why do you think I use the words "temporary obstacles" throughout this book? Help your mind through these challenging times by minimizing the bad. Convince yourself that the hurdles and challenges you may encounter on your journey will be short-lived. Adjectives are your friends—use them to downplay the importance of challenges on your path to your S.M.I.L.E. Use adjectives often—they're cheap, readily available, and a great ally on your journey. By using adjectives that minimize the importance of negative nouns (temporary obstacles, surmountable challenges…), you subconsciously program yourself to interpret challenges, setbacks, and obstacles as temporary.

Affirmations

Affirmations cost just as much as adjectives (they're free). These are positive statements that also serve to reinforce your mind with a positive force. An affirmation is an assertion or a statement. Obviously, I encourage you to enrich your vocabulary with positive affirmations. These are positive thoughts that you repeat to yourself to provide strength, courage, and motivation at opportune times. Don't wait for times of need to call upon affirmations—you can also use them as part of your regular daily or weekly routine.

MORE ON VOCABULARY

Napoleon Hill: Think and Grow Rich

Hill describes the benefits of using affirmations, although the term he uses is autosuggestion. He believes we have the power to program our mind for success by means of autosuggestion. Hill writes, "autosuggestion is the agency of control through which an individual may voluntarily feed his subconscious mind on thoughts of a creative nature, or, by neglect, permit thoughts of a destructive nature to find their way into this rich garden of the mind." He provides examples of using affirmations to focus your mind on your goals and program yourself to expect success. This makes you a machine that's programmed to fulfill your destiny. Using affirmations is a strategy used in the website tools as well.

Listing your objectives and the steps it will take to achieve them focuses your mind on the task at hand. For example, if you wish to lose four pounds in one month, that translates into a loss of a pound a week. Using the website tools, you would indicate that your S.M.I.L.E. is to lose four pounds in one month, or one pound per week. Achieving that objective will take several steps, starting with a proper diet and regular exercise. You'll need to see a positive result when you step on the scale at the weekly weigh-in, losing at least a pound a week to meet your objective in the specified time frame.

Your affirmations would therefore consist of positive statements for each of the steps involved in meeting your objective. Suggest thoughts to yourself, such as "I will eat properly at my next meal" (diet), "I will avoid junk food" (diet), "I will go to the gym today" (exercise), and "I will have a good workout today" (exercise). These are what Hill refers to as autosuggestion and what I call affirmations. You notice that they're all positive in nature, as they involve good things (proper diet, good exercise). These affirmations are food for your brain. They provide positive reinforcement.

The advantage of the website tools is that you agreed to the objective and the steps required before embarking on your quest. Therefore, you can't change your mind midway through your journey and change the rules. If you believe you must lose a pound a week, then you must put in the effort required, such as dieting and exercising, to meet your goal. Luckily, using the website tools makes it easier to move through the steps as there's no improvisation. Once you arrive at the third step of Phase 2 (Managing Your Performance), all you have to do is focus on giving your best efforts to the tasks at hand—diet and exercise, in this example. The affirmations serve to convince your mind that the steps must be taken to fulfill your destiny. All you have to do is walk through the door and deliver.

Solutions

There's a vocabulary problem that's so prevalent in the workplace today that it borders on being an epidemic. If there's one thing I've learned in my business dealings with management in accounting firms and senior executives in public companies, it's that the men and women at the top want to hear solutions—they don't want to hear problems.

MORE ON MENTAL LAZINESS

Robert Kiyosaki - Rich Dad Poor Dad

Kiyosaki frequently criticizes people who suffer from "mental laziness," which he describes as a condition in which people want better things for themselves but aren't willing to invest the mental effort to think of how to get what they want. Kiyosaki cites the example of someone who wants fancy jewellery or an expensive sports car. Despite their desire for these luxury products, people who are "mentally lazy" will distance themselves from their dream rather than use their imagination to devise a method of obtaining them. They will use vocabulary such as "I can't afford it" or "It's too expensive." Sorry, but it's just way too easy to give up on something you really want.

Kiyosaki feels that people paralyze themselves by explaining away the nicer things in life simply because they don't want to "pay the price" by using imagination, creativity, and hard work to pursue their dreams (remember our physics lesson?). His main message is to avoid mental laziness. Nothing positive can possibly come from it. He encourages people to stop saying, "I can't afford it," and instead ask, "How can I afford it?"

My advice is similar. To succeed at finding your S.M.I.L.E., you must shun mental paralysis by keeping your mind focused on attaining your objectives. We've already looked at how vocabulary can help your mind on the journey to success. As we've seen, adjectives and affirmations provide a cheap and readily available boost for your mental faculties. Solutions are another positive influence for your mind.

We all must train ourselves to adopt the reflex of providing solutions, not problems. How often do you hear people around you saying, "We'll never make it," or "That problem is just too difficult," or "The client called and they're really upset"? It's one thing to ask for advice, but it's unforgivable to rely on someone else to fix your problem. It's perfectly acceptable to ask someone for help when you're stuck and you genuinely want to learn how to remedy the problem, but it's quite another case if you're too lazy to think of a solution yourself and expect someone else to bail you out.

Asking someone for help so you can learn and not have to rely on them in the future is excellent. Asking someone else to fix your problem simply because it's easier than doing it yourself doesn't help you in the long term. Furthermore, it traps your mind in a state where you don't use your own problem-solving abilities, since you believe there will always be someone to pick up after you. Everyone is guilty of this sin at some point in their life, so don't despair if you find yourself doing this. However, be aware of the harmful effects.

Training yourself to think of solutions to your own problems is an indispensable skill. Learn to present possible solutions to problems to yourself and those around you. This shows thought. It shows initiative. It shows creativity, imagination, and effort—all qualities that will prove to be indispensable on your quest. Why not learn them immediately? It may be awkward in the beginning if you haven't made a point of this in the past. You'll be amazed at how powerful this reflex can be once you train your mind to brainstorm to find an immediate solution when a problem presents itself. Use this skill and learn to develop it. It will be extremely useful on your journey. There will be times when you have to rely on your instincts to solve a problem.

Conclusion: Vocabulary

The vocabulary you employ in your daily life says a great deal about your character, your attitude, and your will. Use the proactive vocabulary we've discussed in this chapter. Your mind will benefit greatly from the adjectives, affirmations, and solutions that you introduce into your arsenal. They cost nothing but a little time, but they can be extremely effective.

"Many an optimist has become rich by buying out a pessimist."

– Robert G. Allen

"For myself I am an optimist—it does not seem to be much use being anything else."

– Sir Winston Churchill

MIND STRATEGY: POSITIVE THOUGHTS

Preview

- **Positive thoughts are your friends.**
- **Positive thoughts are your mind's allies.**
- **Challenge yourself to think positive thoughts constantly.**

Introduction

There is some overlap between this chapter and the chapter on vocabulary, as positive thoughts have a great deal to do with our discussion on affirmations. This is intentional. It's important to speak positively and use a proactive vocabulary. And it's equally important to think positive thoughts throughout your everyday life. Your thoughts influence your words, which in turn influence your actions. Positive actions, performed repeatedly on a daily, weekly, and monthly basis, will eventually lead you to your S.M.I.L.E.

We all want to do good—for ourselves, our families, and our friends. How can you, though, if you think negative thoughts or use negative vocabulary? Negativity is poison. Don't spread poison to those around you—Justin Timberlake was not the first to say that "what goes around comes around." You reap what you sow. If you share positive vibes with those around you, they will bounce positive vibes back to you, creating a positive "buzz" that will uplift your mind when you're in need of encouragement. Day-to-day life can be challenging at times. Maintaining a positive focus and state of mind will help you achieve your goals and reach your maximum potential. People with a positive, affirmative mentality have a natural drive that's hard to match, unless you do as they do and spread positive karma yourself.

MORE ON THE POWER OF POSITIVE THOUGHTS

Rhonda Byrne: The Secret

Byrne explores the idea that your thoughts have an enormous amount of power in the universe. The author claims that your desires create a "law of attraction" that will give you what you crave. She says that you must absolutely want something and command it in your thoughts and dreams in order to receive it.

Byrne believes that negative events are the result of imperfect thoughts; therefore, those who experience bad things in their lives do so because they project that karma onto themselves. Byrne gives further examples that are too controversial for me to outline in this PG-13 book. The Secret has its supporters and detractors. It should be obvious by now that I firmly believe in the benefits of positive thinking. I also believe that having a negative outlook will reduce your chances of finding your S.M.I.L.E.

Positive Psychology

As a golfer with a high handicap (which means I'm not a very good player), I constantly dwell on the few nice shots I hit in any given round. Those are the shots that make me want to return to the golf course and keep playing the sport. The shots I muff, or send into the forest, or have to play out of mud are definitely not the memories I want to take home from a day at the golf course. Instead, I choose to focus on my good shots. And why not, I paid for the round! Granted, there are times when my friends claim my swing resembles a gardener planting tomatoes. And granted, it sometimes really does feel as though I'm gardening as opposed to playing golf, but I always try to think of my best hits of the day. Positive thoughts rule the sport.

The same applies to parenting, whether you've been at it for six months or six decades. Every parent cherishes those happy thoughts of their children. It's amazing to watch an infant speak those sweet first words, learn how to walk, and eventually grow up to be a young adult. However, as a parent, can you honestly tell me that there were only happy thoughts as your child grew, or were there also times that were very challenging, when you wondered why you ever decided to be a parent?

You know what I mean. Wiping baby bottoms is not the most enjoyable way to spend your day. Waking up in the night to feed a crying baby, struggling through your day sleep-deprived because your baby didn't sleep, attending a parent-teacher meeting to discuss your kid's bad behaviour—none of these are the moments you cherish most as a parent. Yet these things happen, and they're normal. As your child grows up, there will be great times and more challenging times.

When you look back at the experience of raising your children, I bet you'll find that you only recall the good times. This is excellent! And that's what I mean about fostering only positive thoughts. Yes, it's true that life sometimes presents you with good situations, just as it does with bad situations. Which would you rather focus on? Obviously, you only want to remember the good ones. This is what I mean about positive thinking and harbouring positive thoughts. Ignore the negative thoughts, which only make otherwise good situations look worse than they have to. Negativity ruins everything by bringing clouds to your picnic.

Taking Inventory

Sometimes, you don't even have to formulate positive thoughts of where you'd like to be in the future and what you see yourself doing in a few years in order to provide yourself with motivation. It's just as easy and effective to sit back, think about all the things you are grateful for, and take comfort in the fact that you're already a very lucky person.

Taking Inventory ("T.I.") is a strategy I employ very often. It's a simple concept that stresses simplicity, humility, and gratefulness. You'll find it most useful during periods when you question yourself or your abilities. Taking inventory means evaluating your current situation and establishing value.

Companies take inventory all the time. In accounting, we learn that taking inventory is extremely important and should be done on a regular basis. For example, companies with inventory (shoes, purses, cars) must take inventory on a daily, weekly, or monthly basis. Counting the amount of stock in inventory tells management exactly how much product they have on hand, if the goods available in the warehouse are of sufficient quality, and whether they need to re-order more items to meet customer orders. Companies can't survive without taking regular inventory.

The concept of taking inventory is so simple, yet so vital, that its usefulness may easily be overlooked. In our case, "inventory" can be anything.

It doesn't necessarily have to be a product—it could be a quality, a skill, or a personal asset. If you're an honest person (quality), then you have honesty in your inventory. It's something you can "use" to get you something. In addition, taking inventory may also show you talents, skills and abilities you should be grateful to possess. If you're creative (skill), then you have a special skill not everyone possesses. If you have a vast network of influential friends (personal asset), then your inventory includes a group of well-positioned contacts you may be able to tap into for assistance. Therefore, you must T.I. (take inventory) to be aware of what you currently have.

Companies take inventory in various ways. It can be as simple as making a list of all the merchandise in the warehouse and counting the items to make sure the list is accurate in terms of quantities and product types. The next step is the value-added part: management reviews the inventory list and assigns a value to each item. That figure (quantity multiplied by value) tells you how much your inventory is worth. Management then compares the worth of their inventory today versus what it was worth in the previous inventory count. For example, if the jewellery you had in inventory at $175 per unit the previous month is now worth $299 per unit, then the value of your inventory has risen. The only way you can determine this, however, is to T.I.

Your Personal T.I.

The same applies to you. If you're creative, what value do you attribute to your creativity? Can you rely on your creativity to generate the success you seek to achieve? All valid questions. You may not be able to answer them fully the first time you T.I., but you should be able to assess the value of your personal inventory the next time.

How do you know where you're going if you don't know what you have in your possession that can take you there? What if you have something, but you're not sure whether it's of sufficient quality? Also, if you don't have what you need, how can you expect to use it when a temporary obstacle arises? T.I. will help. It obliges you to stop, assess your skills, talents, and qualities, and assign a value to them. It forces you to think. It takes effort to evaluate things. It's much easier to "go with the flow" and leave everything to chance. It's much more fun to "take it as it comes" and "take a chance." You must take the time to T.I. You must know what you have. The benefit of performing this self-evaluation is that not only does it let you identify what you possess, but it also highlights what you don't have.

For example, if you notice you're extremely technical but not very creative, perhaps you may have to invest some time in developing a creative skill. Or perhaps you want to rely solely on your technical ability and ignore the creative side altogether, realizing you'll need someone else's help on all creative matters. This would be the case for someone who's skilled in performing detailed analyses, but lacks originality on the artistic side.

It's important to realize that there are no wrong answers when you T.I. There is no teacher waiting to grade you and tell you what you got wrong. This exercise should serve as an informative strategy to determine your assets. It will let you know what you have, and hopefully, what you need. The benefits to be derived from T.I. lie in what you do with the information. To simply T.I. without utilizing the results of your assessment is worthless. The first step is to T.I. The next step is to evaluate the results and make informed decisions (with your personal inventory listing, you are "informed"). You may decide to rely on some of your strongest assets, qualities, or skills, or get more help in areas in which you feel there are some gaps.

If you want to be a successful musician and your self-evaluation highlights the fact that you're skilled with instruments, yet you're shy and not a skilled promoter, then you're lacking in the "sales" aspect. Obviously, musical talent is a good quality to have if you want to be a successful musician. However, being able to promote your concerts and CDs will also have an impact on your musical success. Therefore, based on your T.I., you may either have to develop your sales skills (through books, seminars, and courses) or hire a manager who can promote your skills. The only way to be in a position to determine this is through T.I.

Isn't it comforting to know you have a talent or a skill in your arsenal? It should give you some confidence to know you have an ally you can rely on when you need to. If you consider yourself to have good sales skills, it's important to officially establish the skill as a key asset on which you intend to rely to promote yourself or your product. The only way to formally identify all your assets is to evaluate yourself, and most importantly, conduct periodic reassessments to make sure that what you believe you possess actually exists, and you can count on it in the future.

T.I. can also be used to list all the good things in your life. Isn't it comforting to know that your T.I. shows you have excellent athletic skills, you're blessed with a fantastic family, and you have several friends you can count on, regardless of the circumstances? Private, personal reflection is the only way to determine all your strengths, weaknesses, and opportunities. There will be times on your journey when you need quality time with yourself to perform this self-assessment. Make sure to use the results of your assessment to bolster your thoughts in a positive sense.

Conclusion: Positive Thoughts

Use positive thoughts on your journey to find your S.M.I.L.E. They will provide the necessary support for your mind to combat fear. Maintain a positive attitude and success will be yours. "Count your blessings" is more than just a song title.

BODY STRATEGY: DIET AND EXERCISE

Preview

- **Get very friendly with both diet and exercise.**
- **Both diet and exercise make your body feel great.**
- **Incorporate diet and exercise into your mission.**

Introduction

Welcome to another feel-good strategy for your body! North Americans seem to be spending more and more of their thoughts, efforts, and consumer dollars on addressing health issues. It reassures me to see more and more people thinking about their health, the foods they eat, and the consequences of not caring about diet and exercise.

On a recent trip to Europe, I was amazed to see how advanced Europeans are when it comes to diet and exercise. We've all heard the (positive) stereotypes, and there's a best-selling book called French Women Don't Get Fat. Well, neither do Italian women. Based on a totally unscientific study, with no proper sampling (translation: I observed Italian passersby in the street from my vantage point in various espresso bars), I came to the conclusion that Italians, and possibly Europeans in general, have incorporated proper eating and lifestyle habits that promote good health into their daily lives.

I was amazed at the amount of walking Europeans do. In Rome and in small Italian villages, everyone seems to go for a long walk after lunch and especially after dinner. Many Italian workers have to rely on public transit and walking to work and home again, which is a much more practical alternative than sitting in chaotic traffic jams. So Italians (and other Europeans) walk much more than we do. Expensive gas that costs more than two to three times what North Americans pay is one reason why many people choose to walk, along with lack of parking and dangerous traffic in large European cities. Europeans benefit from their walking, since it is an excellent form of exercise.

When I use the term "diet," I don't mean a deprivation diet that you follow for a few weeks or a few months. I mean the foods you eat all the time. Italians don't believe in "going on a diet" or in "give us one week and we'll take off the weight." There's no such thing as a "magic pill" that miraculously helps you lose weight. Italians eat properly at every meal: fruit, vegetables, meat, fish, and grains, olive oil, no butter or margarine, a little sugar at dessert or in their coffee, wine, and believe it or not, ice cream. They eat very little fried food, few French fries, and no processed foods. Nearly everything they eat is fresh. In fact, everything you serve them had better be fresh or they'll refuse to eat it. By North American standards, Europeans are fussy eaters—they won't eat just anything, and they insist on high-quality ingredients. Their serving sizes make our portions look enormous by comparison. Yet, given the low incidence of obesity and how attractive they are, young women and men alike, I believe they must be doing something right.

Diet and Exercise: What It Does

Physical health puts your body on track to support your mind as you embark on your journey to reach your full potential and achieve success. Remember the strategy for your mind that involved positive thinking? Positive thoughts are the fuel for your mind. Diet and exercise provide fuel for your body. It's vital to nourish your body with high-quality fuel. In information technology, the concept of "garbage-in garbage-out" is universally accepted: the better the input, the better the output. Feed your body a steady stream of healthful foods, give your body plenty of exercise, and be amazed at the power you'll unleash from within yourself (or as one of my favourite motivators says, Awaken the Giant Within). You already know that your body is a living, breathing organism, so make sure you care for it, nurture it, and let it grow. Take care of your body and it will take care of you. A healthy body, combined with a healthy mind, will yield an unstoppable force.

Diet

You must eat properly. No arguments. A true diet does not mean short-term sacrifice—it means permanent healthy eating habits. Furthermore, I believe a healthy diet takes precedence over exercise. Exercise alone will not give you a healthy body. I have known many people who exercised regularly yet ate poorly and could not stay slim. Diet comes first, exercise second, but you need both for the "perfect marriage." One cannot exist without the other. I hope I can convince you of the benefits of a healthful diet and demonstrate how it benefits your body on your quest for success.

A healthy diet will make you feel good. If you feel good, then you'll perform well. You must perform well in order to satisfy your personal objectives. You won't get to your destination with an empty fuel tank.

I do occasionally eat in restaurants. However, I do prefer to cook my own meals, which is cheaper, healthier, and gives me complete control over the ingredients, freshness, and quality. Meals don't have to be complicated. There are millions of guides out there on the market (books, magazines, and websites). I adore the Mediterranean diet of olive oil, bread, cheese, simple carbohydrates (pasta), proteins, fish, and wine. In addition, I use light spices (salt and pepper) to enhance the flavour of my meals. I am an advocate of the Michel Montignac diet, among others, but I despise the Atkins diet (I refuse to give up my carbs). The South Beach diet is cool and has helped many members of my family. With a little research, you'll find meal plans that work for you and your loved ones. If Mediterranean-style cuisine interests you, I encourage you to visit Europe and/or the western part of the Middle East for inspiration. Of course, my favourite is Italian cuisine (my mother would disown me if I stated otherwise).

One last anecdote about my recent trip to Italy. My wife and I were amazed at the simplicity of most of our meals in Europe. Sandwiches were one slice of cheese and one slice of ham. There was no butter or mayonnaise in the sandwich, but it was grilled to melt the cheese. It was delicious. On another occasion, we dined in a mozzarella bar. We sampled ripe buffalo mozzarella with tomatoes, parsley, a spoonful of pesto sauce, and some grilled vegetables, along with a bottle of white wine. We were thrilled with our tasty meal and left the place extremely satisfied.

Eating doesn't have to be complicated, but you must monitor portion size. This is the single most significant difference between North American and European cuisine. Europeans eat smaller quantities. They savour their food, while we devour our meals. Europeans take pleasure in taste and flavour.

We super-size our meals and equate satisfaction with quantity. We have to change this and learn to be satisfied with smaller quantities of better quality food. You owe it to yourself to eat nothing but the best food. Forget about those shiny rims for your Escalade and spend more on groceries. I assure you it will make your future meals much more enjoyable and improve your health.

Quick quiz: name something I feel very strongly about, spend quality time with on a daily basis, and cherish greatly. If your answer was "my wife," you'd be correct based on the way I described it, but no, I was talking about coffee. I love coffee. It makes me feel good. I'm an Italian-Canadian, so coffee is as much a part of my routine as wine, bread, cheese, and pasta. Coffee is an important part of our social rituals—every visit involves having coffee together—and not just any kind of coffee, but the good stuff.

I drink one or two espressos every day. The second one usually puts me over the top. Sometimes I substitute a latte for my morning espresso, depending how I feel. I'm very, very picky about my coffee. Price doesn't matter—what counts is the quality. I refuse to drink free coffee from those office machines. My European roots compel me to value good quality stuff: "If a thing's worth doing, it's worth doing it well"—or not at all.

Italians in Italy are fortunate because there's excellent coffee to be found everywhere: around the corner, at the train station, at the airport … everywhere. A latte is nice when you have more time and feel like sipping a drink that has warm milk in it. Espresso is nice because it has very few calories and you don't have to heat up milk, or even add chocolate or cinnamon sprinkles.

Coffee can help you on your mission to find your S.M.I.L.E. The caffeine is what does the trick. According to WebMD.com, "caffeine is a commonly used drug that increases alertness, decreases fatigue, and improves muscle coordination. Though coffee comes to mind as the most common source of caffeine, it's also naturally found in tea and chocolate, and it is often added to soft drinks and non-prescription medications like pain-relievers and cold remedies."

For now, let's focus on coffee—sorry, tea-lovers. I prefer coffee to soft drinks or energy drinks because it's a more natural product. I do occasionally drink soft drinks, but I rarely have energy drinks. Although soft drinks and energy drinks contain significant amounts of caffeine, coffee comes from the earth in the form of coffee beans and does not contain manufactured chemicals. Drink coffee because it's natural and it can help your body on your quest to capture your S.M.I.L.E.

Caffeine boosts alertness, which helps you focus and concentrate while you're performing the steps you need to execute to succeed. We've already discussed the temporary obstacles you will encounter on your journey. Heightened concentration and alertness will help you stay focused on your goals and lessen your fear of hurdles you may find in your path.

My morning coffee signals the start of my day. It's part of my daily routine and it tells my body that we're getting ready to tackle the challenges ahead. A pre-exam coffee provides that extra boost of energy/confidence/chutzpah I need to perform at my peak level. I always made sure to have at least one coffee on exam days throughout my undergraduate and post-graduate studies, and throughout my summer preparatory studies in the weeks leading up to my Canadian Chartered Accounting exam. Don't overdo it on caffeine, though, because too much gets your heart rate racing and if you aren't used to the sensation, it won't feel pleasant while you're writing your exam. I believe a little caffeine in your diet (preferably in the form of coffee or tea) will prove to be beneficial, and your body will thank you for it.

Of course, you don't have to drink a coffee before doing anything in the course of your day—you don't want to become addicted. A simple coffee is one of life's simple pleasures, helping you get you through your day. Caffeine also has a positive effect on your confidence because it boosts your heart rate. It will make you breathe better, feel better, and perform better.

According to the Health Canada website (www.hc-sc.gc.ca), everyone but children and pregnant women can safely consume up to 400 milligrams of caffeine per day. This translates into approximately four espressos, three regular cups of coffee, or eight cups of tea. One or two coffees a day will not cause problems for most people and can definitely improve your performance.

There are many places in North America that offer good quality coffee. I suggest going to the Little Italy in your city for the real stuff. If this is not feasible, go to any European restaurant (preferably Italian or French), where there will be likely be an espresso machine. Of course, if you're in

Manhattan, you're reasonably sure to find a coffee shop three steps away. In Manhattan, you don't even have to cross the street to go to the coffee shop on the other side—just walk a few more steps and you're bound to find another.

Enjoy coffee, but in moderation. If you overdose on caffeine, you could become one of those latte monsters who always have a cup in their hand, consume countless coffees per day, and nod their head up and down with such ferocity (from all the caffeine) that they could knock a hole in cement. People who are over-caffeinated can come across as annoying, so bear with me. I consume a moderate amount of coffee on a daily basis, so I'm in the mid range. Did you see the skit on Saturday Night Live with the characters who work in a coffee shop? That's what I mean about those coffee-abusers.

Coffee is an important part of your diet. Both Health Canada and the FDA (U.S. Food and Drug Administration) approve of reasonable caffeine consumption. I prefer to get my caffeine through coffee or tea, but soft drinks or energy drinks will do if you can't find a good coffee shop. Coffee will help your body deal with the hurdles you may face on your journey by boosting alertness, concentration, and heart rate. This is one of my favourite strategies. I hope you enjoy it, too.

Exercise

Exercise is another way of doing good for your body. Diet and exercise combined are two simple yet effective means of staying fit and making sure that body remains in optimum condition.

Exercise doesn't have to be glamorous. Your body doesn't care whether you wear a designer outfit or a cheap T-shirt. It won't exercise any differently if you opt for an expensive membership than if you exercise by walking and jogging on the sidewalk. What's important is to incorporate regular physical activity into your routine at least three times a week. It's important for you to be in optimal physical condition so that you can show the world the most attractive "you" possible, stay physically strong, and have a body that can withstand the challenges you'll encounter on your way to your S.M.I.L.E. Remember, a healthy mind and a healthy body are the most effective weapons in your arsenal.

Any kind of exercise will benefit your body. Exercise boosts your heart rate, gets your blood flowing, and works your lungs and your muscles. Exercise also burns calories. If you make a healthy diet part of your lifestyle and you exercise regularly, you will soon reap the physical rewards and achieve excellent physical health. Exercise will also boost your confidence level and help relieve stress (remember when I said the strategies are best used combined?). If you exercise properly and exert yourself, your body will produce and release endorphins. Endorphins produce pleasure, so don't be surprised if you feel really, really good after a solid workout.

The benefits of exercise have been documented at length in countless books and magazines. I've never seen an advanced society as aware of our health as we are today in North America, but many people fail to apply that knowledge. There are so many options available for anyone who wants to get into shape and have fun. All you have to do is get going. I know it's difficult to find the time to exercise, but it's up to you to make the time. Be practical and use your imagination! Don't forget, walking on your lunch hour or after dinner counts as exercise. Cycling with your spouse and children also counts. Don't forget about that weekly dance lesson with your partner—that counts as a workout too. There are so many things you can do to keep in shape. Challenge yourself and you'll be amazed by how well your body responds. Regular exercise will make you feel fantastic and give you additional leverage as you strive to be your best.

Conclusion—Diet and Exercise

You need your body to be in top shape to succeed in your mission. Build a healthy diet and regular exercise into your mission. You can keep it simple, but once you make diet and exercise part of your daily routine and lifestyle, you'll be amazed how great they make your body feel and how dramatically your performance improves.

BODY STRATEGY: STRESS RELIEF

Preview

- **Stress relief is an important skill to learn.**
- **Stress is a temporary obstacle.**
- **Using the strategies in this step will help minimize stress.**

Introduction

Not a day goes by without another scientific study, poll, or opinion survey on stress. North Americans are increasingly feeling over-stressed. There's a multitude of reasons for this epidemic. Obviously, ever-increasing demands at work play a significant role in the prevalence of stress in our lives. With cell phones, e-mail, and Blackberries, are you ever really "out" of the office? And then there's our insatiable appetite for more disposable income to pay for bigger homes, newer clothes, and fancier cars. All that (plus the cost of living) adds up to a record number of households in which both spouses work outside the house on a full-time basis. As a consequence, there's less quality time for couples to relax, enjoy each other's company, and get intimate since more urgent needs like meals, child care, and child-related activities are shared by both working spouses.

Stress can take a serious toll on your mind and body while you're on your personal mission to achieving your S.M.I.L.E. Stress is your enemy. I had to deal with stress on numerous occasions in my quest to graduate, and chances are that you'll encounter this temporary obstacle as well. Let's look at what happens to your mind and body during a stress attack. The techniques I describe here involve physical action, so you'll use these strategies to reinforce your body. If you experience stress on your journey, and you use these techniques, your mind will also benefit. In fact, this chapter could also come under the heading of mind strategies.

Stress: A Temporary Obstacle

Stress is a temporary obstacle that manifests itself in various forms: tension, anxiety, or panic attacks. Stress is a delicate subject because it can be difficult to recognize. Stress doesn't always formally introduce itself, present a business card, and ask if it can return at a more opportune time. It's not like a blow to the body that hurts immediately, leaves a bruise, and heals over time. It's a state of heightened anxiety, as your heartbeat quickens and you feel a general sense of unease.

Some people thrive on this feeling and say it's the only way they can function. I am not one of those people. I don't like anxiety, dread, or panic. I've dealt with stress for most of my academic and professional career. I've seen enough stress to realize that it's not your friend, it influences both mind and body, and it also affects your decision-making abilities. I have seen people do some bizarre things under stress. Stress is present everywhere in today's society, it's entirely normal, and dealing with stress is vital to your mission.

Basically, stress plays on your fears. You can be doing fine on your journey to find your S.M.I.L.E. when all of a sudden, you feel that change in momentum that I described in the confidence section. Stress then makes its appearance known by metamorphosing into fear, panic or dread. Now, instead of continuing on your progress, you find yourself facing an unknown enemy (fear/panic/anxiety) that has taken precedence over everything else you were in the process of doing. It's normal to feel as though your body is suddenly under attack. It's acceptable to feel a mild anxiety coming on. This occurs when you're doing something you care about and you start to worry about your performance, your actions, or the consequences of the current task at hand. So don't be too hard on yourself for feeling stress—it's a normal physiological reaction to a stimulus in your environment. This is your body's spider-sense tingling, warning you of a possible danger. It's entirely up to you to calm your mind and body, reassure yourself, and return to a state of calm so that you can continue your work.

<u>Anthony's True Confession No. 6:</u> ***I suffer from stress and panic attacks, but I've learned successful coping and control strategies.***

My stress levels would manifest themselves the same way over and over again. I'd feel myself getting nervous at school or work, and my neck and shoulder area would get tense. This uncomfortable tension would persist until the blood flow in my neck and shoulders was so restricted I'd get a headache. The headache was a signal to my body to calm down because the cause/effect relationship was complete.

I wasn't stressed any more, but now I had a headache to deal with that came about as a result of the tension. When I had a headache, I'd have trouble concentrating, trouble speaking, and a general feeling of fatigue, so of course my performance would suffer. My headaches would usually last until I went home, took a pain-killer, and lay down to rest. I always woke up the next day feeling better, but I'd have lost half a day of productivity.

I also began to suffer panic attacks midway through my undergraduate career at McGill University. My panic attacks came and went, but remained a temporary obstacle I had to deal with on the way to my S.M.I.L.E.

Eventually, I learned to control both the tension headaches and the panic attacks. These temporary obstacles were under control by the time I took my final Chartered Accounting exam. Only after I succeeded did I take the time to evaluate exactly what would happen before my episodes of despair and analyze the circumstances in order to find a solution. Obstacles like stress make things messy. They're not life-threatening, except in certain extreme cases, but they do hamper your performance—and we're all interested in improving our performance by becoming successful performance managers, correct?

After deep introspection and reflection, I was able to determine what circumstances led to the stress. I already had a general idea of what was causing it during my academic career, and I was able to deal with these panic attacks on a short-term basis. However, I knew that I had to conquer this enemy if I wanted to live a panic-free existence and be as productive as I could.

I realized that the tension in my neck and shoulders that led to tension headaches was caused by situations in which I perceived deadlines or imminent failure, or was having to deal with pressures that were beyond my control. For example, I often felt tension at work before I graduated and obtained my C.A. designation. This was not my employer's fault; it was my own fault for letting myself feel that way. Yes, my workload was significant, challenging, and demanding, but it was up to me to manage my performance well enough to meet my obligations to my employer, clients, and team-mates.

I eventually learned to handle deadlines once I gained more experience. My immediate superiors also made it clear that I needed to set deadlines to plan current and future mandates. However, they also told me that if ever I felt a deadline was unfair, I should discuss it with them to see if alternative arrangements could be made to ease the burden. Direct communication alleviated some of my personal pressure.

It also dispelled the perception that management didn't care ("perceived pressure"). They did care, but it was up to me to let them know how I was feeling and arrive at a mutually beneficial solution. All of a sudden, I had only my fear of failure to deal with. Between coffee, confidence, positive thinking, and stress-relief strategies, my fear of failure quickly disappeared, leaving me tension-free. I am happy to say I learned a lot in those years before finding my S.M.I.L.E., and I've continued to learn every day. I rarely suffer tension headaches today, so I can proudly say that, although I still get nervous from time to time, this obstacle became temporary. To this day, it remains a minor obstacle in my daily life, allowing me to perform at my full potential.

I knew the consequences of my panic attacks all too well—I failed many exams because of them. Sometimes my rapid breathing and feeling of paranoia made sitting in a classroom unbearable. My panic attacks occurred whenever I felt anxious, pressured, or uncomfortable in class, even if I had friends next to me or I was surrounded by other classmates. They didn't happen every day, but I had them frequently during midterms and exams. The bouts would last for several minutes, forcing me to get up from my desk and leave the classroom to get some fresh air.

The downside to this was that I would have to leave the classroom for several minutes, even during an exam. So while my classmates were completing their exam I was outside, breathing deeply, waiting for my heart and lungs to settle down. I would end up wasting precious time and not doing as well on the exam as I could have. This sometimes meant that I failed a class and had to re-take it the following semester. Obviously, I wasn't thrilled with this scenario, but I had to endure this temporary obstacle until I figured out a solution.

The panic attacks were the result of feeling that I was not in control of a situation. You can imagine how dreadful this feeling was for me, a self-professed control freak. I wouldn't feel in control during exams that tested me on subject matter I hadn't studied. I wouldn't feel in control in classes where I was significantly behind on my reading. And I wouldn't feel in control when I felt tired, since that was when my fears (fear of failure, risk, and change) would come back and challenge me.

The strategies in this book helped me conquer my panic attacks. My main ally in eliminating panic attacks was confidence, which I developed by practicing hard and working harder. I felt a sense of panic whenever I was faced with new material on an exam, when I was behind in my work or felt tired. It was easy to remedy the problem once I had pinpointed the sources of my discomfort. With practice, I developed more confidence. I began to study not only the assigned material, but other material as well. Now I knew more about possible "surprise" subject matter that the professor might put on the exam. This simple solution helped me learn to "think outside the box" and be prepared for anything. It also minimized my anxiety at being faced with unfamiliar material on an exam. I knew I'd have to be resourceful and flexible. The method wasn't foolproof, but it was the best way to prepare myself for whatever I might face on the exam.

I also became much more disciplined with my assignments and readings so I never fell too far behind in my studies. Now I was keeping up with the class, which gave me the luxury of focusing on subject matter that I believed I needed to re-study at the end of the semester. Again, this strategy helped keep my panic level to a minimum. Finally, I adopted a regular study schedule that became a routine. I incorporated frequent breaks and rest periods into my routine to make sure I was well rested. This also reduced my anxiety level. Through hard work, practice, and positive thinking, I learned to control my stress levels so I could perform at my maximum potential.

My allies in my war on panic attacks were all of the strategies in this book (confidence, vocabulary, positive thoughts, coffee, diet/exercise, and the stress-relief strategies in this chapter). These useful techniques, which are highly effective when combined, can help you through challenging times. Make them part of your daily routine. Combining them makes them all the more powerful.

Remember the Transformers, that cartoon from your childhood? The Constructicons were always more powerful combined with Devastator. Omega Supreme was always more powerful when combined, than when he was a rocket base with a rocket, tank, and train track. The Dinobots were formidable allies to the Autobots, and even more powerful as a team rather than on their own. Wasn't Sex and the City funnier when Miranda, Charlotte, Carrie, and Samantha were all together? Combine good things and you can conquer anything.

Stress Relief: Solutions

It's important to learn strategies for keeping your stress levels down during your quest. I was able to self-diagnose my panic attacks and tension headaches because I know myself very well (most migraine sufferers do). Stress, panic, fear, and hysteria are all under your own control. A doctor or psychologist can show you techniques you can use to calm yourself down, but it's up to you to cure yourself of that feeling of doom.

The best advice I was ever given on stress levels was at a three-day seminar while I was working for a Big 4 accounting firm in Montreal. We learned effective breathing. It doesn't have to be any sexier than that: breathing. The counsellor who addressed the audience of Chartered Accountants and business consultants coached us through an exercise that involved closing our eyes, breathing deeply for several minutes, and focusing on inhaling, exhaling, and the sound of her soothing voice. The entire room was silent. All you could hear was about 100 people breathing heavily in unison, which was oddly relaxing.

That technique (breathing slowly) was worth its weight in gold. I have used the deep breathing technique on many occasions, at work, before bed, or any other time I feel overwhelmed. The technique involves inhaling and exhaling very, very slowly. I remember the seminar leader saying it was very important to focus on your breathing, trying to inhale and exhale for as long as you could. Doing this for several minutes clears your mind and leaves you in a state of relaxation in which all you focus on is your breathing. This is the most effective relaxation tool.

Now I understand why yoga is so popular. Try it when you feel overwhelmed, on your break, or when you're trying to get to sleep, and you'll be amazed at the sense of calm that will come over your body. This shows how a strategy for your body can also benefit your mind, because your thoughts will also turn to your breathing, setting aside your problems and worries.

Rest and Relaxation

Getting proper rest is another strategy that often overlooked in a world that's on the move 24 hours a day, seven days a week. Telecommunications, electronics, and non-stop entertainment (shopping, clubs, and after-hour parties) keep us busy all day long and into the night. The downside to this "always on the go" society is that we actually forget to rest. We need to train ourselves that downtime is not only acceptable but necessary. It takes more than one vacation a year to rest properly. I don't consider a one-week holiday in the Caribbean to be adequate rest, as you'll return to the same jungle you left behind.

Factor rest (proper sleep) into your lifestyle to let your body recover and your brain function properly. It's extremely difficult to eat properly, concentrate, and do anything effectively on four hours of sleep. Incorporating regular sleep patterns into your routine to ensure that your body, and ultimately your mind, are both in peak condition is the only way to conquer your fears and achieve your S.M.I.L.E. Learn to sleep properly at night for six to eight hours, depending on your needs. That doesn't mean you can't go out partying, but do realize that sleep deprivation is real and won't help you achieve your goals. Sure, it's fun to go out and stay up late, but you may need to sleep in the next day to recover. This is normal. Sleeping is not one of the original sins, so don't feel guilty if you feel the need to rest.

I know that my confidence level is at a low (and my stress levels high) when I haven't slept properly and I feel pressured to perform. I've survived meetings at work when I hadn't had much sleep the night before, but you won't be able to deliver your best performance consistently when you're sleep-deprived.

Building proper rest and relaxation into your routine will make you ready to face the challenges involved with finding your S.M.I.L.E. Your body will thank you and reward you for taking its needs into consideration. Better yet, you'll keep your stress levels in check and focus on your performance.

Conclusion: Stress Relief

Stress may prove to be a temporary obstacle you have to deal with on your path to success. Stress relief solutions can be as simple as deep breathing, proper rest, positive thinking, and appropriate confidence-building exercises. Armed with the strategies discussed in this book, you'll find stress relief a straightforward and extremely useful tool once mastered.

"Whenever I hear, 'It can't be done,' I know I'm close to success."

– *Michael Flatley*

"Criticism is prejudice made plausible."

– *H.L. Mencken*

"Pay no attention to what the critics say... Remember, a statue has never been set up in honour of a critic."

– *Jean Sibelius*

Step Four: Managing Your Environment

TEMPORARY OBSTACLE: NEGATIVE REINFORCEMENT

Preview

- **Negative reinforcement stinks.**
- **Negative reinforcement is the second most important temporary obstacle in your path to success.**
- **Learn to recognize negative reinforcement and deal with it effectively.**

Introduction

I hope you've noticed that I constantly look at the positive. I always try to employ affirmatives when I speak and write. I love the word "yes" and hate the word "no." I adore using positive adjectives and I hate negative thoughts. I've stressed the importance of positive thoughts, words, and actions—effective tools as you prepare to wage war with negative forces. Negative thoughts and words are like a cancer that can spread if left unchecked. I hope you're mentally and physically prepared for your next temporary obstacle: negative reinforcement.

Negative Reinforcement

Negative reinforcement is any negative thought, word, or action from someone else. I say "someone else" because I know in my heart that at this stage of your S.M.I.L.E. conquest, you've incorporated the strength of positive thoughts, words, and actions into your routine. That's why this chapter is in Step 4: Managing Your Environment. You already know how crucial it is to stay positive at all times. Now it's time to focus on conquering your environment (those around you).

Here are some common examples of negative reinforcement:

"You can't do that."

"You won't be able to do this."

"You won't be able to sell that."

"No one will believe you."

"No one wants that."

"Nobody will ever pay for that."

"You aren't___________enough" (fill in the blank: smart, pretty, handsome, big, small, old, young…)

Negative reinforcement takes many different forms and aliases. However it chooses to manifest itself, it's dangerous, and you need to be prepared. Negative reinforcement is so mischievous that it can sometimes find a way to spoil your S.M.I.L.E. just as you're about to claim your success once and for all. Although I consider fear your primary temporary obstacle, negative reinforcement is in second place, but just as lethal because it can hit you even after you've conquered all your fears. You may still be vulnerable to negative reinforcement.

At this stage, the challenge lies not within you, but around you. In The Matrix (my favourite movie), Morpheus takes Neo on a tour of the virtual training simulator in which they're walking on a busy city street. Morpheus is easily wading through the human traffic while Neo struggles to keep up with him. The pretty woman in the red dress walks by Neo, drawing his attention to her good looks until Morpheus recaptures his attention and tells Neo to look closely at her once more. When Neo turns around, he's shocked to see an agent holding a gun to his face less than a metre away.

Morpheus tells the team to halt the simulation, leaving Neo in awe of what just transpired.

That agent in the simulation is negative reinforcement. It sneaks up on you and points its weapon at you while your guard is down, leaving you totally exposed. Don't let negative reinforcement get that close to you. Recognize its dangers and acknowledge that it's poison. Just as Morpheus successfully trained Neo to never let his guard down and trust his instincts while in the matrix, do the same when you're faced with negative reinforcement so you can continue on your path to success.

People who say any of the common negative phrases listed above should be ticketed by the police for a negative reinforcement infraction. The statements say nothing, prove nothing, and mean nothing—unless you let them; this is precisely why negative reinforcement is a temporary obstacle. It can only get in your way if you let it.

Negative reinforcement can come from any source. Morpheus tries to tell Neo that their threat can come from anywhere and look like anybody (office worker, passer-by, or a pretty woman in a red dress). Realize that negative reinforcement is similar—it may originate from anyone in your life: strangers, acquaintances, colleagues, or even family. Have any of these people ever planted a seed of doubt in your mind by using one of those negative phrases? Those phrases won't encourage you to pursue your dreams; in fact, they cast doubt and despair onto your dreams.

Have you ever confided your plan to do something spectacular to someone only to have the person immediately tell you why "you can't do that" or "that won't succeed"? How many times have you heard one of those negative phrases? How does hearing that someone doesn't think you're capable of doing something make you feel? I bet it makes you feel saddened, dampens your spirit and perhaps even makes you start to doubt yourself. It's tragic and unfair to throw water on the fire to douse someone's flame, yet it happens every day. How many ideas never leave the drawing board because someone criticizes the idea and makes the owner feel that there's no chance of success? Negative reinforcement is a real and serious threat to your mission to S.M.I.L.E. Recognize that fact and accept negative reinforcement for what it is: nothing more than someone's negative opinion.

Everyone has the right to their opinion, of course, just as you have an equal right to yours. You may wonder how it's possible that your friends, colleagues, or even family members could purposely sabotage your ideas by negatively reinforcing your ideas and dreams. Well, negative reinforcement in any form, originating from any source, has a terrible effect on your hopes, dreams, and desires. It serves only to discourage you from reaching your full potential. There are jealous people out there who would love it if you were to stay where you are and not succeed—so that they look better by comparison. People like this have nothing positive to contribute.

Friends and family may sometimes provide unknowing negative reinforcement. They may be the ones to tell you their doubts about your ideas, but just because they do that doesn't mean they don't love you. It may just be how they were raised, and they're simply stating the first thought that comes to mind. Not everyone who negatively reinforces you is your enemy. Some people just don't know that they shouldn't be spreading negative thoughts, through ignorance or lack of empathy or support for those around them. I want you to hate the negative reinforcement itself, not the person who sends it your way. Realize that there's absolutely nothing to be gained from negative reinforcement, regardless of the source.

The unfortunate thing about negative reinforcement is that sometimes it's the first instinctive reaction for many of us. I know many people who are only trained to see the flaws in certain things. I know many people who, if you were to present them with an idea (a product, service, or some other suggestion), would only be able to give you a long list of reasons why your idea won't succeed. The tragedy is that they wouldn't be able to see the opportunity, benefits, or rewards of a new idea. Imagine going through life criticizing everything around you—how can anyone find pleasure with this bad habit ingrained in their mentality?

MORE ON NEGATIVE REINFORCEMENT

Robert Kiyosaki: Rich Dad Poor Dad

Kiyosaki also believes that it is vital to ignore any negative messages people send you, and learn to deal with others' negativity and fears. He believes that people who say things like "you can't do that" or "you won't be able to accomplish this" aren't really talking about you at all—in fact, they're talking about themselves. What they're really saying is not that you can't do it, but that they can't do what you want to do. They simply can't see—mentally—how they could possible do the thing you want to accomplish. Whatever you call it, people do sometimes say negative things, and you need to realize what they're really saying.

Negative Reinforcement: Anthony, What Should I Do?

Don't listen to these people who have only negative things to say—they're ignorant, jealous, or don't know any better. It is your mission, as part of your quest to find your S.M.I.L.E., to ignore their negative messages, whether they're purposely trying to discourage you or they haven't learned the benefits of seeing opportunities. In any case, it points to a lack of class, lack of knowledge, and lack of appreciation for others. This is not your fault, so don't ever blame yourself for their actions.

It would be a kind gesture to inform people who negatively reinforce others of the consequences of doing so and how they should seek to encourage rather than discourage others. Of course, they may well disregard your advice and continue to be negative, in which case they've made their choice and will have to live with the consequences of having a negative outlook. Be patient with people who can't see the good in life. Always be kind, courteous and respectful to them, despite the seeds of doubt they plant in others. As a civilized person, all you can do is show everyone the same respect and politeness, but you're well within your rights to ignore their negative messages. Pay them no attention. This does not diminish you in any way; in fact, it shows patience, class, and maturity to deal with others' negativity and carry on in a dignified manner. You can do it. And you'll grow as a person once you perfect this skill and use it regularly.

Conclusion: Negative Reinforcement

Train yourself to recognize negative reinforcement. Train yourself to ignore it, for it serves no purpose. In his music, 50 Cent makes countless references to "player haters" (people who hate, people who cast doubt). Ignore the player haters, who won't help you on your journey but only seek to ruin your fun and discourage you from achieving your S.M.I.L.E.

Negative thoughts only ruin your trip to success. Don't pack negative feelings, thoughts, or actions in your luggage as you voyage towards your S.M.I.L.E. Leave them behind and enjoy the trip.

"Call it a clan, call it a network, call it a tribe, or call it a family: Whatever you call it, whoever you are, you need one."

– Jane Howard

"Happiness is having a large, loving, caring, close-knit family in another city."

– George Burns

"In every conceivable manner, the family is a link to our past, a bridge to our future."

– Alex Haley

ADDITIONAL STRATEGY: FAMILY

Preview

- **Your family loves you.**
- **Your family includes your spouse, friends, and acquaintances who would love to see you succeed.**
- **Use this positive source of inspiration to successfully find your S.M.I.L.E.**

Introduction

I loved the movie My Big Fat Greek Wedding, though I'm not big, fat, or Greek. I'm sure anyone with any idea of the trials and tribulations of having a family relates to the movie, regardless of what corner of the globe you originate from. Family can be funny at times. Family can be annoying at times. However, family remains family, and it's a powerful force in the universe. Family ("famiglia" in Italian) is the first of three strategies in this section. Despite what George Burns says above, I love my family and I know they love me. I simply like teasing them, as in the quote. Whatever tough love I give my family is returned in kind.

Why Is Family Important?

Family can also play a role in your quest for success. Family represents a variable in your environment; used properly, your family can be a source of inspiration, strength, and wisdom. Family represents people around you who care for you, love you unconditionally, and are ready to help you should the need arise.

Take courage in the fact that there may be times during your journey to success when you'll be in need of companionship. There will be times when temporary obstacles spring up and make life temporarily difficult for you. At such times, use the strategies discussed in Step 3 - Managing Your Performance - success comes from within. However, a warm, loving family can make an important contribution to your life. With family comes responsibility—don't take family for granted. You must be supportive, respectful, and loving to cherish your family and love them as they love you. Sometimes this is easier in theory than in practice. But as with your S.M.I.L.E. journey, the rewards make it worth the trip.

You're an extension of your parents, who in turn are the children of your grandparents. You've inherited traits from both sides of your family. Have you ever asked them to share the lessons they learned growing up? Have you ever asked your parents about their experiences? You could discover things you never knew about them. Perhaps your parents and grandparents had their own dreams of success as you do now. What can they tell you to shed light on your current path to success?

I love my parents and I love my grandparents. They've blessed me with many gifts I hope I'll be able to pass on to my own children and grandchildren. Yes, there are days when I take my parents and grandparents for granted. However, I've always had excellent communication with my parents and grandparents, and that makes me grateful for everything I have. I enjoy every moment with them. Since my grandparents only speak Italian, I was encouraged to study at the elementary and university level to learn their language, visit Italy with them, and follow sports and politics in Italy—all of which has definitely brought us closer.

My parents speak English, so there was never a language barrier. They're also fairly knowledgeable about pop culture and all the latest electronic gadgets, which bridges the generation gap and makes it much easier for us to relate to each other. Due to our closeness, I feel I can speak freely to my parents and rely on their help in times of need. Having support from above (from your elders) is priceless. Having your family's support should boost your confidence and help you seek your maximum potential in everything you do.

A spouse and siblings can also provide wonderful support. A spouse is someone you can trust, confide in, and turn to whenever you need help. A spouse is a life partner you want to grow with, share life's joys with, and possibly have children with. These are important steps in anyone's life. Family makes you realize that there are special people you can share your success with once you do achieve your goals. Your siblings also give you love and support, since you've spent most of your young life growing up alongside them. These are people who know you well, have watched you grow up, and will always be there for you. Consider your siblings and spouse sources of inspiration to draw from as you seek out your S.M.I.L.E.

Friends and acquaintances are also part of your extended family. Don't discount the richness of having friends from the same or different origins as you. Whatever their backgrounds, they too provide support, friendship, and inspiration in times of need.

In my quest for my S.M.I.L.E., I learned a lot about myself through my interaction with everyone in my extended family: my spouse, parents, siblings, grandparents, and friends. My family gave me the extra support I needed to find my S.M.I.L.E. and obtain the Canadian Chartered Accounting designation. It was a long journey, but I knew it would end in happiness and success that I could share with my family. I knew that when I graduated, I would organize a party with all my supporting cast (my family) to celebrate reaching this important milestone in my life. I kept my promise, succeeded, and promptly organized a party to celebrate with everyone who had helped me overcome the challenges.

Conclusion: Family

Draw on the strength of your family to inspire you, support you in times of need, and help you find your S.M.I.L.E. and achieve your success.

"If our country is worth dying for in time of war let us resolve that it is truly worth living for in time of peace."

-Hamilton Fish

ADDITIONAL STRATEGY: CULTURE

Preview

- **Your culture is part of your identity.**
- **Your culture includes your language, customs, and traditions.**
- **Use this positive source of inspiration to successfully find your S.M.I.L.E.**

Introduction

Culture represents the second of the three strategies in this section. Your culture is part of who you are as a person. The journey to your personal success will teach you a great deal about yourself. It will be an opportunity to learn as much about yourself, your environment, and life in general as you can. My journey took many years, very little blood, much sweat, and a few tears. I'm happy to have seized the opportunity, since I now find that I know myself much better.

Why Is Culture Important?

I was born in Montreal, Quebec (Canada), the descendant of Italian immigrants. I am extremely proud of my heritage as a Canadian of Italian origin. I have traditions that are genuinely Canadian along with those from my Italian background. In addition, I speak Canadian French, since I hail from the province of Quebec. And I have other peculiarities typical of Montreal residents: the habit of switching from English to French in mid-sentence, poor driving skills, and occasional cravings for smoked meat and bagels. Montreal is a multicultural city, a melting pot of many different cultures. Living here has taught me not only about my unique culture, but about many other cultures too.

What does your culture tell you about traditions and customs? How well do you know your culture? What challenges does your cultural identity face in the future? Are there opportunities for your culture that you're aware or unaware of? There's an ancient Chinese proverb that says, "know thyself, know thy enemy." The strategies in this step deal with learning more about everything around you. Although this chapter focuses on environment—factors that are external to you and all around you (family, culture, and religion)—they still have an impact on who you are as a person inside. Do you see the link? As all these external factors relate to what's internal to you, it's worthwhile investing some time in learning more about your culture and further clarifying your identity.

This chapter isn't long because, like the chapter on family, it is personal. This chapter is meant to remind you that your cultural identity matters because it plays a role in defining who you are as a person. If nothing else, learning more about your culture will help you develop additional self-confidence that you can employ on your journey. Every culture in the world has something positive to contribute to mankind. It's your responsibility to learn what is unique and genuine in your culture, incorporate it into your quest, and use that knowledge accordingly.

Conclusion: Culture

Invest an appropriate amount of time in learning about your culture. Learning more about yourself and your community will prove to be a priceless and personally enriching experience.

"Desire, ask, believe, receive."
– Stella Terrill Mann

"Human beings must be known to be loved;
but Divine beings must be loved to be known."
– Blaise Pascal

"Whatever God's dream about man may be, it seems
certain it cannot come true unless man cooperates."
– Stella Terrill Mann

ADDITIONAL STRATEGY: RELIGION

Preview

- **Your religion is also part of your identity.**
- **Your religion affects your beliefs, customs, and traditions.**
- **Use this positive source of inspiration to successfully find your S.M.I.L.E.**

Introduction

In addition to your family and culture, your religion also represents part of who you are as a person. It's part of your identity. Religion, faith, or beliefs (whatever you want to call it), is an important and often neglected aspect of your life. In our fast-paced society, sometimes it seems that who will win the next Dancing With the Stars competition or which member of Good Charlotte Hillary Duff will date next is more important than faith. Whether the fault lies with the media, which devote unlimited attention to Hollywood celebrities, or with our society for continuing to read the tabloids, it seems that we've forgotten how important faith can be in our lives.

I am by no means a model Roman Catholic, so I don't want to come across as too "preachy." I realize that religion and faith are very personal. I respect the fact that there are countless other religions out there (Christianity, Judaism, Islam, Buddhism, Atheism…). It's entirely up to you to decide which religion you feel most comfortable with. I made my choice growing up and I encourage you to practice in your own way.

Why Is Religion Important?

Not only is religion a useful way to find your S.M.I.L.E., it can also help you with your life, creating a sense of purpose and providing a deeper meaning. It can help you deal with difficult situations in life, clarify your stance on moral issues, and give you hope and an ideal. Religion gives you a "best-practice" on how to live your life and highlights what you can look forward to in your lifetime. Does religion work for everyone? Probably not. However, it does provide a system of values, adds meaning to your thoughts, words, and actions, and for many, creates a sense of safety and security.

I believe religion can help keep you focused on other less material things. Religion provides an opportunity to reflect on everything you have to be grateful for in life. It tells you that you're not alone in this world. Faith creates a sense of community, since people from your neighbourhood come together at least once a week to pray together and listen. It encourages private reflection and introspection. It may also motivate you to spread good vibes and positive thoughts to everyone you may encounter that day and for the rest of the week.

I always feel good when I attend Sunday mass, though I don't go as often as I should, because it's time I spend away from work, my laptop, and my Sony Playstation and focus on other, less material things. I'm not a model Catholic, but I do know that religion has a role to play in my life. Whether you use religion and worship as a way to live your life or simply as an escape from the modern world, I believe it should play some role in your life. It feels great to have a sense of purpose and direction. Of course, religion doesn't provide all the answers. It won't cure you of all your troubles, make that cute guy/girl in class like you more, or make you a better investor, but it can help. Having faith won't fix the noise in your muffler, but it can add some value to what you feel in your mind, body, and soul, and help you become a better person.

Faith is a piece of the puzzle. It can add that extra something that you are looking for. How you choose to include religion in your life is a very personal decision and nobody can tell you how you should do it. When you do incorporate religion into your life, in your spouse's life, and in the lives of your family and friends, you will likely feel a joy that was not there previously. Learning more about your beliefs and your faith will help you grow as a person and discover things you weren't aware of previously.

There are certain core beliefs in the Roman Catholic faith that I like very much: kindness, forgiveness, and charity. Kindness means treating other people as you would like to be treated. Forgiveness means accepting and moving beyond whatever wrong others have done that is contrary to your interests. Charity means giving back to your church, your community, and those around you. Religion provides a positive message for anyone who's willing to listen.

Kindness and charity are two values that are paramount when dealing with success. Believe it or not, what you do after you succeed is just as important as investing all the time and effort in attaining success. What are the core beliefs in your faith, and what can you learn about your religion? What positive messages can you incorporate in your quest for success?

Conclusion: Religion

Religion can mean different things for different people. Each religion has something positive to contribute to humanity. In a world of electronic gadgets, 24-hour satellite television, and wireless Internet, it's very easy to forget about the contribution religion can make to our lives. Establishing religion as part of your life will make you feel good and add greater meaning to your life and your mission to succeed. I also know, based on my own experience, that it will make your S.M.I.L.E. all the more worthwhile.

"You always pass failure on the way to success."

– Mickey Rooney

"Success is the ability to go from one failure to another with no loss of enthusiasm."

– Sir Winston Churchill

"Many of life's failures are people who did not realize how close they were to success when they gave up."

– Thomas A. Edison

Phase III: S.M.I.L.E.ing (Smiling)

Welcome to Phase III

Welcome to your success! This is where you prove that you can accomplish anything if you persevere long enough. This is where you enjoy the fact that you've been successful in the planning and execution of your S.M.I.L.E. strategy. This is where your dreams come true.

This phase is the most special because by now, you've not only planned your mission, but actually executed it according to your initial plan. You are now a certified success story! It's time to enjoy the fruits of your labour. In Phase III, you reflect on all you've been through, the efforts you've expended to get here, and the joy that you and your entourage (your spouse, family, and friends) are feeling right now as everyone toasts your success.

This unforgettable journey has taken a great deal of will power and energy. You now have all the knowledge and tools you need. Now let's do an ESPN-style Top 10 recap of the steps in achieving your S.M.I.L.E.:

1) Get everything started (Step 1).

2) Define your S.M.I.L.E., which makes your objectives official (Step 2).

3) Manage the performance of your mind and body and reject fear, using all the strategies outlined in this book (Step 3).

4) Manage your environment (Step 4) and make it conform to your needs and objectives, using the further strategies in this book.

5) Arrive with your newfound S.M.I.L.E. (Step 5) and get ready for what comes next.

Your journey can end right here if you want it too. You can put down this book and go out with your friends to celebrate, since you are now an official success. But first, let's consider your success. What remains to be done? How do you make sure this ecstasy you're now feeling doesn't fade away? Let's look at how you can savour the feeling of S.M.I.L.E.ing and keep it forever.

"There is only one success—to be able to spend your life in your own way."

– Christopher Morley

"We succeed only as we identify in life, or in war, or in anything else, a single overriding objective, and make all other considerations bend to that one objective."

– Dwight D. Eisenhower

"If you wish success in life, make perseverance your bosom friend, experience your wise counselor, caution your elder brother and hope your guardian genius."

– Joseph Addison

Step Five: You've Found Your S.M.I.L.E.

NOW WHAT?

You've Found Your S.M.I.L.E.

Congratulations on your victory. I hope that having achieved your personal S.M.I.L.E. is as enjoyable and amazing as you imagined it would be. It's been a long and hard road to travel, but as my favourite proverb puts it, "The end justifies the means." So now your journey is over and there's nothing left for you to do—or is there?

What you do with your success once you achieve it can be just as important as the road you took to get here. Obviously, having achieved success is a great feeling—enjoy it. It's certainly more fun to look back and reminisce about having succeeded than to be at the other end working towards your goal at an early stage of your quest. Looking back, you can see that each phase in your journey involved important goals and challenges. Phase I involved the challenge of planning your mission—dreaming a dream, desiring the successful completion of an objective, and clearly defining the exact nature of your objective. Phase II represented the grunt work.

Phase II required the successful execution of your strategy. This was the most challenging part and introspective part of your journey. I'm certain that by the end of Phase II, you had learned things about yourself you didn't know before.

If Phase I was the most fun and Phase II was most challenging, then Phase III is the most rewarding. Phase III requires you to do two things:

1) Enjoy your S.M.I.L.E.

2) Share your S.M.I.L.E. with others.

In Spider-Man, Peter Parker's uncle tells him "with great power comes great responsibility." That applies to you as well. You're now a success. You've found your S.M.I.L.E, and you possess something special. Now it's time to give back. It's time to share your success and help others.

"There is no duty more obligatory than the repayment of kindness."

– *Cicero*

Your responsibility is to share your newfound success/wealth/happiness with other people. How you do so is entirely up to you. If your S.M.I.L.E. involved amassing a certain amount of wealth, then choose an amount to give to charity. Society will benefit regardless of how much you give. You could make a donation or set up a foundation that will benefit current and future generations. If your S.M.I.L.E. was to be a superstar recording artist like Justin Timberlake, help make a young artist's dream come true by helping him or her to become a professional singer too. If you chose to be an exceptional professional athlete, then consider using your newfound image not only to sign lucrative endorsement deals but to volunteer your celebrity status to help young children. Little ones always need a hero to look up to. There are positive role models in the world but there's always room for more. Be a "big brother" or "big sister" and help guide kids along a path of personal development. Volunteer your time to an organization that helps others. No contribution, in time or money, is too big or too small. Every contribution counts and serves to make society a better place.

"The best thing to give to your enemy is forgiveness;
to an opponent, tolerance; to a friend, your heart;
to your child, a good example; to a father, deference;
to your mother, conduct that will make her proud of you;
to yourself, respect; to all men, charity."

-Francis Maitland Balfour

I'm not a billionaire and I don't command a multi-million dollar salary, but I'm grateful for the interesting, challenging, and rewarding work involved in chartered accounting. I'm also grateful for the fact that my wife and I earn a comfortable living. We both volunteer our time and donate regularly to our favourite charities. Colleagues, friends, and family frequently seek our help in our professional capacity. We do this freely and willingly, and constantly look for ways to do more.

MORE ON GIVING BACK

Robert Kiyosaki: Rich Dad Poor Dad

Stories of people giving back any way they can are always inspirational. Kiyosaki's books focus on creating, accumulating and maintaining wealth, but he also believes in the charitable aspect—giving back. Obviously, you can't give everything away since you need to go on living and providing for your family and loved ones. However, Kiyosaki challenges his readers to give back in for the general benefit of the community. He cites examples of superstars like Warren Buffett, Bill Gates, and Richard Branson as humanitarians and philanthropists and inspiring examples of highly successful people who have accomplished incredible things and chosen to share their gifts with those who are less fortunate. However, you don't have to look to billionaires for inspiration—there are people in your city right now who also contribute regularly in any way they can to charity. The important thing to realize is that it's great to enjoy your success, but don't forget about sharing your success with others to help them reach their full potential too.

One of the major reasons why I chose to write this book was to use it as a way of inspiring my readers and showing that underdogs can win in the long run. I've always enjoyed writing and communicating, whether by telephone, e-mail, and face-to-face. The main message of this book is that regardless of your DNA, last name, and genetic makeup, you can achieve what you want in life. I struggled throughout my academic career, with frequent failures and disappointments. However, graduating successfully was a very sweet achievement for me, and I encourage you to use the steps outlined in this book to make your dream come true. Whether this book makes the best-seller list or not, I will continue working hard at everything I do, and my wife and I will continue to share and give back to those who are less fortunate than we are.

Challenge yourself and explore your full potential. I am totally convinced that the steps outlined in this book can help you reach your goals. Use this book to plan, execute, and enjoy your S.M.I.L.E.

I am certain you will find your life much more rewarding and meaningful, and that once you attain and share your S.M.I.L.E., you will experience greater happiness than you have ever known before.

I wish you courage, good luck, and all the best.

"Happiness is when what you think,
what you say, and what you do are in harmony."

-Mahatma Gandhi

Appendix I

ANTHONY'S S.M.I.L.E. DOCUMENTS

Website Tool: Personal Guarantee

Date: September 1, 1994

I, Anthony Pennimpede, have a personal goal: To become a Canadian Chartered Accountant in the province of Quebec.

This personal goal represents my S.M.I.L.E.

This agreement is to certify that I, Anthony Pennimpede, personally guarantee myself that I will find my S.M.I.L.E. regardless of the time, effort and sacrifice required to obtain it.

I will accomplish this with the help of my book Finding Your S.M.I.L.E., www.AP3media.com, and the website tools.

I believe I will find my S.M.I.L.E. by December 31, 2003.

I also guarantee that once I find my S.M.I.L.E., I will do all I can to enjoy it, take care of it, and share it with those closest to me.

Signed: Anthony Pennimpede - signature

Website Tool: Objectives

Your S.M.I.L.E.:

To become a Canadian Chartered Accountant in the province of Quebec.

Does your S.M.I.L.E. represent one objective or many objectives?

List your objective(s):

Obtain Chartered Accountant designation

Website Tool: Steps Needed to Complete Objectives

Your S.M.I.L.E.:

To become a Canadian Chartered Accountant in the province of Quebec.

Does your S.M.I.L.E. represent one objective or many objectives?

List your objective(s) and the steps needed to complete the objectives:

1. Objective: Obtain Chartered Accounting designation.

    Step 1: Graduate from college: obtain commerce degree

    Step 2: Graduate from university: obtain undergraduate bachelor of commerce degree

    Step 3: Graduate from university: obtain graduate diploma in public accountancy

    Step 4: Successfully complete the Canadian Institute of Chartered Accountants' UFE (Uniform Final Examination)

Website Tool: Completion Certificate

Date: December 16, 2003

This is to certify that Anthony Pennimpede successfully found his/her S.M.I.L.E. on December 16, 2003.

Anthony Pennimpede indicated on the Personal Guarantee that his/her S.M.I.L.E. was to become a Canadian Chartered Accountant in the province of Quebec. Therefore, this completion certificate is granted unconditionally to Anthony Pennimpede in recognition of all the work, sacrifice and dedication demonstrated in finding his/her S.M.I.L.E.

CONGRATULATIONS!

Signed: Anthony Pennimpede - signature

Marquis Book Printing Inc.

Québec, Canada
2007